Mediterranean Diet Cookbook

100+ Delicious, Easy, and Healthy Recipes for Everyday Cooking - 28-Day Meal Plan for Weight Loss Challenge

Thomas Teselli

Copyright © 2019 Thomas Teselli

All rights reserved.

TABLE OF CONTENTS

Introduction xiI

Chapter 1: The Mediterranean Diet Concept 1

Chapter 2: Delicious Breakfast Options 7

    Baked Eggs & Zoodles With Avocado 7

    Basic Crepes 8

    Breakfast Egg Muffins 9

    Broccoli & Cheese Omelet 10

    Chia Berry Overnight Oats 11

    Crustless Spinach Quiche 12

    Deep Dish Spinach Quiche 14

    Delicious Scrambled Eggs 15

    Egg White Scramble With Cherry Tomatoes & Spinach 16

    Eggs Baked In Tomatoes 17

    Feta Frittata 18

    Feta-Quinoa & Egg Muffins 20

    French Toast Delight 21

    Greek Omelette Casserole 22

    Herb-Sausage & Cheese Dutch Baby 23

    Holiday Breakfast Sausage Casserole 24

    Low-Carb Keto Egg & Ham Muffins 26

Mediterranean Omelette 27

Mediterranean Toast 28

Peanut Butter & Banana Greek Yogurt Bowl 29

Poached Eggs 30

Potato Hash With Poached Eggs, Chickpeas, & Asparagus 31

Pumpkin Pancakes 33

Quinoa Egg Breakfast Muffin 34

Shakshuka Classic 35

Spanish Potato Omelet 36

Vegan Gingerbread & Banana Quinoa Breakfast Bake 37

Watermelon Feta & Balsamic Pizza 39

Chapter 3: Healthy Lunch Options 40

Arugula Salad 40

Chickpea Salad 41

Cucumber Salad 42

Fruity Curry Chicken Salad 43

Honey Lime Fruit Salad 44

Insalata Caprese II Salad 45

Nicoise-Style Tuna Salad With Olives & White Beans 46

Shrimp Orzo Salad 47

Tomato Feta Salad 48

Zesty Quinoa Salad 49

Zucchini, Artichoke, & Chicken Salad 50

Chicken Soup 51

Chickpea Garbanzo Soup 53

Creamy Italian White Bean Soup 54

Fast Seafood Gumbo 55

Greek Lentil Soup 57

Lemon Chicken Soup 58

Quinoa Soup 59

Red Lentil Soup 61

Vegetable Noodle Soup 62

Fasolakia - Green Beans & Potatoes 63

Fried Rice With Spinach, Peppers, & Artichokes 65

Hummus & Prosciutto Wraps 66

Linguine With Garlicky Clams & Peas 67

Quinoa Black Bean Burger 68

Skillet Gnocchi With White Beans & Chard 69

Sweet Slaw 71

Chapter 4: Favorite Dinner Choices 72

Chicken & Orzo Pasta 72

Chicken Breast Cutlets With Capers & Artichokes 73

Chicken Sausage Gnocchi Skillet 75

Feta Chicken Burgers 76

Grecian Pasta Chicken Skillet 77

Italian Chicken Skillet 78

Lemon Chicken Piccata	79
Lemon Chicken Skewers	81
Quick Chicken Marsala	82
Sicilian Olive Chicken	83
Slow-Cooked Lemon Chicken	84
Slow Cooked Mediterranean Roasted Turkey Breast	86
Super Tender Chicken	87
Avocado & Tuna Tapas	88
Baked Salmon With Dill	89
Feta Shrimp Skillet	90
Flounder - Mediterranean Style	91
Halibut & Capers	92
Lemon Garlic Shrimp & Veggies	93
Pan-Seared Salmon	95
Penne with Shrimp	96
Salmon With Warm Tomato-Olive Salad	97
Scallops Provencal	98
Spanish Moroccan Fish	99
Tilapia Feta Florentine	101
Greek Honey & Lemon Pork Chops	102
Grilled Pork Loin	103
Mediterranean Pork Chops	105
Chicken-Fried Steak	106

Mediterranean Farfalle 107

Mixed Spice Burgers 108

Philly Cheesesteak Sandwich With Garlic Mayo 110

Roasted Veggie Pasta 111

Sweet Sausage Marsala 112

Chapter 5: Snack Favorites 114

Chocolate Almond Butter Fruit Dip 114

Date Wraps 115

5-Berry Compote With Orange & Mint Infusion 115

Greek Baklava Bars 117

Pistachio No-Bake Snack Bars 119

Yogurt & Olive Oil Brownies 120

Garlic Garbanzo Bean Spread 121

Spiced Sweet Roasted Red Pepper Hummus 122

Chapter 6: Delicious Desserts 124

Baked Quince With Cinnamon 124

Chia Greek Yogurt Pudding 125

Finikia 126

Frozen Mint Greek Yogurt 128

Greek Butter Cookies 129

Greek Cheesecake With Yogurt 130

Greek Honey Cake 131

Greek Lemon Cake 132

Greek Yogurt Bowl With Peanut Butter & Bananas 134

Greek Yogurt Chocolate Mousse 134

Honey-Pistachio Roasted Pears 135

Honey Pistachio Tart 136

Italian Apple Olive Oil Cake 138

Low-Fat Apple Cake 140

Popped Quinoa Crunch Bars 141

Pumpkin Bread 142

Raspberry Fudge Greek Frozen Yogurt 143

Strawberry Greek Frozen Yogurt 145

Sweet Ricotta & Strawberry Parfaits 146

Triple-Chocolate Tiramisu 147

Watermelon Cubes 148

Smoothies For All Times 149

Green Avocado & Apple Smoothie 150

Healthy Breakfast Smoothies Variety Pack 151

Mediterranean Smoothie Delight 152

The Ultimate Breakfast Smoothie 153

Chapter 7: Your Special 29-Day Meal Plan & Pyramid Food Options 155

The Pyramid Options 169

How to Maintain the Mediterranean Diet Plan 171

Conclusion 176

MEDITERRANEAN DIET COOKBOOK

Introduction

Congratulations on purchasing your *Mediterranean Diet Cookbook*, and thank you for doing so. I am so excited that you have chosen to take a new path using the Mediterranean way of eating. Before we proceed, here's a bit of history.

Ancel Keys, a scientist, and his colleagues, including Paul Dudley, who later became President Eisenhower's cardiac physician, conducted a *Seven Countries Study* in the years following World War II. The study compared individuals in the United States to those living in Crete, a Mediterranean island. Keys examined the plan, testing people of all ages using the Mediterranean Diet.

The study examined 13,000 middle-aged men in Finland, the United States, the Netherlands, Yugoslavia, Greece, Italy, and Japan. It became evident that fruits, vegetables, grains, beans, and fish were the healthiest meals possible, even after the impoverishment of WWII. All of these discoveries were just the starting point.

Many benefits will be discussed, including how you can lose and maintain a healthy weight in a sustainable way. Each chapter will carry you through different aspects of the plan and how you can go about changing your eating patterns with the Mediterranean diet.

You will also discover that while on the Mediterranean diet plan, you will have more energy, and with that energy, you can become more active. Motivation will be the leader as you head toward your new lifestyle, making essential changes along the path to success. Now, it's time to learn how to use the techniques of the Mediterranean Diet Plan.

After you have the basics, you will enjoy a 28-day menu plan with all the recipes included. You even have one bonus day to start off the following week. Each item suggested on the plan has the calories, carbohydrates, protein, and total fats listed. It cannot be much easier than this.

So, Let's Get Started!

Chapter 1: The Mediterranean Diet Concept

Foods You Can Eat

Dairy Products: These items contain calcium, B12, and Vitamin A: Greek yogurt, regular yogurt, cheese, plus others are beneficial.

Eggs: Duck, quail, and chicken eggs.

Seeds and Nuts: Source of minerals, vitamins, fiber, and protein: Macadamia nuts, cashews, pumpkin seeds, sunflower seeds, hazelnuts, chestnuts, Brazil nuts, walnuts, almonds, pumpkin seeds, sesame, poppy, and more.

Vegetables: Another excellent choice for fiber and antioxidants: Cucumbers, carrots, Brussels sprouts, tomatoes, onions, broccoli, cauliflower, spinach, kale, eggplant, artichokes, fennel, etc.

Fruits: Excellent choices of vitamin C, antioxidants, and fiber: Peaches, bananas, apples, figs, dates, pears, oranges, strawberries, melons, grapes, etc.

Healthy Fats: Avocado oil, avocados, and olives are excellent fats. The monounsaturated fat, which is found in olive oil is a fat that can help reduce the "bad" cholesterol. Oil has become the traditional fat worldwide with some of the healthiest varieties.

You will still need to pay close attention when purchasing olive oil because it may have been extracted from the olives using chemicals or possibly diluted with other cheaper oils, such as canola and soybean. You need to be aware of refined or light olive or regular oils. The Mediterranean diet plan calls for extra-virgin olive oil because it has been standardized for purity using natural methods, providing the sensory qualities of its excellent taste and smell. The oil is high in phenolic antioxidants, which makes *real* olive oil beneficial.

Whole Grains: Whole grain bread and pasta, buckwheat, whole wheat, barley, corn, whole oats, rye, quinoa, bulgur, and couscous.

Legumes: Provide vitamins, fiber, carbohydrates, and protein: Chickpeas, pulses, beans, lentils, peanuts, and peas.

Red Meats: You are allowed red meats, including lamb, pork, and beef in small quantities. They are rich in minerals, vitamins, and protein—especially iron. Use caution because they do contain more fat, specifically saturated fat, compared to the fat content found in poultry. Don't leave it out entirely; save it for a special dinner or with a stew or casserole.

White Meats: White meats are high in minerals, protein, and vitamins, but you should remove any visible fat and the skin.

Seafood and Fish: Mussels, clams, crab, prawns, oysters, shrimp, tuna, mackerel, salmon, trout, sardines, anchovies, and more.

Poultry: Turkey, duck, chicken, and more.

Potatoes: You receive potassium, Vitamin B, Vitamin C, and some of your daily fiber nutrients. You must consider that they do contain large amounts of starch that is quickly converted to glucose, which can place you at some risk of type 2 diabetes. Use simpler methods of cooking, including baking, boiling, and mashing them without butter.

Black Pepper: Pepper promotes nutrient absorption in the tissues all over your body, speeds up your metabolism, and improves digestion. It can boost fat metabolism by as much as 8% for up to several hours after it's ingested. As you will see, it is used throughout your healthy Mediterranean recipes.

Cayenne Pepper: The secret ingredient in cayenne is capsaicin, which is a natural compound that gives the peppers the fiery heat. This provides a short increase in your metabolism. The peppers are also rich in vitamins, effective as an appetite controller, smooths out digestion issues, and benefits your heart health.

Make Healthier Food Choices by Making Substitutions

- *Breadcrumbs:* You can still enjoy the crunchiness by replacing regular breadcrumbs with crushed pork rinds. The good news is that the pork rinds have zero carbs. Next time, enjoy healthier fats.

- *Pasta:* Replace pasta using zucchini. Use a spiralizer, and make long ribbons to cover your plate. It is excellent for many dishes served this way. For example, you can also prepare spaghetti squash for regular spaghetti.

- *Tortillas:* Get ready to say no to this one, which weighs in at approximately 98 grams for just 1 serving. Instead, enjoy a lettuce leaf at about 1 gram per serving. You will still have a healthy crunch to enjoy!

Macronutrient Explanation

Macronutrients are nutrients, including carbohydrates, fats, and protein that provide energy or calories which are required for your body to maintain your daily body functions and activities. There are three essential macronutrients: fats, proteins, and carbohydrates. According to WHO Eastern Mediterranean Region, the food habits aren't the same in all countries.

In low-income countries, the daily caloric intake is insufficient. Cereals contribute 60% to 80% of total calorie intake based on a 2000 kcal and 2300 kcal dieting scale. In intermediate-income countries, cereals are consumed by more than half of the calories consumed, resulting in a calorie intake ranging between 2700 kcal and 3000 kcal. Fat consumption has increased in several countries and contributes 20% to 25% of the daily energy supply.

Benefits of the Mediterranean Plan

You will enjoy eating natural foods. The Mediterranean diet is low in sugar and processed foods. You can certainly appreciate a diet or a way of life that is close to nature, especially if you can locate some locally produced organic sources. People in the Mediterranean enjoy the same types of delicious desserts, and many are made using natural sweeteners such as honey.

Your vision will improve. You might be able to stave off or even prevent the risk of macular degeneration, which is the primary cause of eyesight loss among adults over 54. The condition affects over ten million Americans, destroying the area of the retina, which is responsible for clear vision. The vegetables and fish with omega-3 fatty acids are the sources that lower or reduce the risk of acquiring this condition. Also, you will have less chance of getting cataracts with the consumption of green, leafy veggies that contain lutein.

You will drop the pounds using healthier practices. Your search is over if you are seeking a worthwhile plan. The Med Plan, as it is sometimes called, has been proven to work for weight loss easily and naturally with its many nutrient-dense foods. The focus is placed on healthy fats to keep the carbs moderately low and improve high-quality proteins. The healthy fats, protein, and fiber keep you much more satisfied than candy, chips, or cookies. The veggies make up the bulk of the meal by filling your stomach. You will not be hungry an hour after your meal, and you won't receive a spike in your blood sugar.

The Mediterranean Plan has helped those with diabetes. The Mediterranean Diet controls excessive insulin, which is a hormone that controls your blood sugar levels. The well-balanced diet that is low in sugar and contains healthy fatty acids can create a balance, so your body can burn off the fat and give you more energy at the same time.

The diet is considered lower in saturated fat but higher in fat than the American standard diet plans, according to the *American Heart Association*. The combination is usually 20-30% quality protein foods, 30-40% healthy fats, and 40% complex carbs. This creates the balance to keep your hunger under control and ease weight gain, which is an excellent way to keep insulin levels normalized.

Reduction in Parkinson's risk factors has been observed. The risk of the disease is cut in half because the high levels of antioxidants in the diet prevent oxidative stress, which is the cell-damaging process. Parkinson's disease affects the cells in your brain, which produces dopamine. You may have some issues with gait and speech patterns, tremors, and muscle rigidity. The Mediterranean diet can help safeguard you from this disease.

Risk factors for Alzheimer's are reduced. Research has deemed that a 40% reduction occurs among those who use the diet plan, and the risk factors associated with Alzheimer's. Dementia can be treated with medication and aided by the Mediterranean plan. You should also consider some additional exercise to slow the process.

You will experience improved agility. Studies have shown that up to 70% of the seniors who are at risk of developing frailty and other forms of muscle weakness have reduced the risks factors using the diet plan.

Improved asthma symptoms are evident from those using the plan. Numerous studies have revealed that the antioxidant diet helped children who followed the plan, emphasizing the intake of plant-based foods and a lower intake of red meats.

As a result, with the energy levels up, so should your mood. Sugar is usually consumed through dessert, fruit, or wine. The balance also prevents the "highs and lows" which is a mood-altering factor. Most individuals on the plan will eat a balanced breakfast within 1 or 2 hours from the time the day starts, which is the time of day where the lowest levels of blood sugar are present in the healthy fats and fibers, along with three meals each day to maintain the balance.

Chapter 2: Delicious Breakfast Options

Baked Eggs & Zoodles With Avocado

Serving Yields: 2

Nutritional Count (each portion):
- Calories: 633
- Carbs: 27
- Protein: 20
- Total Fat: 53

Ingredients Needed:
- Zucchini (3)
- Olive oil (2 tbsp.)
- Black pepper & Kosher salt (as desired)
- Eggs (4 large)
- Avocados (2 halved and thinly sliced)
- *For the garnish:* Red-pepper flakes & fresh basil
- Nonstick spray

Preparation Instructions:
1. Warm the oven until it reaches 350° Fahrenheit.
2. Prepare a baking tin using a coating of cooking oil spray.
3. Use a vegetable peeler to prepare the noodles.
4. Toss the zucchini noodles and olive oil to combine in a mixing container and season to your liking using the pepper and salt.

5. Scoop into four even portions and arrange on the baking sheet. Shape each slice into a nest.
6. Gently crack an egg into the center of each nest.
7. Bake until the eggs are set or about 9 to 11 minutes. Garnish with red pepper flakes and basil.
8. Serve alongside the avocado slices.

Basic Crepes

Serving Yields: 4
Nutritional Count (each portion):
- Calories: 216
- Carbs: 25.5
- Protein: 7.4
- Total Fat: 9.2

Ingredients Needed:
- Eggs (2)
- All-purpose flour (1 cup)
- Water (.5 cup)
- Milk (.5 cup)
- Salt (.25 cup)
- Melted butter (2 tbsp.)

Preparation Instructions:
1. Whisk the flour and eggs together. Slowly, blend in the milk and water. Fold in the butter and salt. Whisk until smooth.
2. Warm up a skillet or griddle using the medium-high temperature setting.

Lightly oil the pan/griddle.
3. Pour .25 cup of the batter for each crepe.
4. Tilt and swirl the pan to prepare the crepe until the first side is lightly browned (2 min.).
5. Gently flip and cook the second side. Enjoy hot.

Breakfast Egg Muffins

Serving Yields: 2 (3 per serving)
Nutritional Count (each portion):
- Calories: 308
- Carbs: 8.7
- Protein: 24.4
- Total Fat: 19.4

Ingredients Needed:
- Cooking oil spray (as needed)
- Eggs (3 large)
- Skimmed milk (2 tbsp.)
- Grated parmesan cheese (4 tbsp.)
- Leek (.33 cup)
- Baby spinach (.75 cup)
- Red pepper (.25 cup)
- Tomato (1, seeds removed)
- Salt and freshly ground pepper (as desired)
- *Also needed:* 6-count silicone or aluminum muffin tin

Preparation Instructions:

1. Spritz the muffin tin with cooking oil as needed.
2. Warm the oven to 375° Fahrenheit before baking time.
3. Whisk the parmesan cheese, eggs, and milk together in a pouring jug.
4. Finely chop the spinach, leek, red pepper, and tomato.
5. Mix all the veggies into a bowl and portion into the six muffin cups.
6. Pour the egg mixture into each cup. Mix it in with the chopped vegetables.
7. Divide the grated cheddar cheese, topping between each of the cups.
8. Bake using the center rack of the oven until the egg is set or approximately 15 to 20 minutes.

Broccoli & Cheese Omelet

Serving Yields: 4

Nutritional Count (each portion):
- Calories: 229
- Carbs: 5
- Protein: 15
- Total Fat: 17

Ingredients Needed:
- Fresh broccoli florets (2.5 cups)
- Large eggs (6)
- 2% milk (.25 cup)
- Salt (.5 tsp.)
- Pepper (.25 tsp.)
- Grated Romano cheese (.33 cup)
- Sliced pitted greek olives (.33 cup)
- Olive oil (1 tbsp.)

- *Optional garnish*: Shaved romano cheese & minced fresh parsley
- *Also needed:* 10-inch ovenproof skillet

Preparation Instructions:

1. Set the oven temperature to broil.
2. Arrange a steamer basket in a saucepan. Pour in about 1 inch of water. Toss the broccoli into the basket. Wait for it to boil.
3. Lower the heat to simmer for 4 to 6 minutes with a lid.
4. Whisk the milk, eggs, pepper, and salt. Toss in the broccoli, olives, and grated cheese into the mixture.
5. Prepare the skillet using the medium heat setting and add the oil. Dump in the egg mixture. Simmer for 6 minutes.
6. Place the skillet in the oven approximately 3 to 4 inches from the heat. Bake until the eggs are set or for 2 to 4 minutes.
7. Move the skillet to the countertop to cool for about 5 minutes.
8. Slice into wedges. Sprinkle using the parsley and shaved cheese.
9. *Note*: The posted nutritional values do not include the optional cheese.

Chia Berry Overnight Oats

Serving Yields: 1

Nutritional Count (each portion):
- Calories: 526
- Carbs: 78.8
- Protein: 15.3
- Total Fat: 17

Ingredients Needed:

- Chia seeds (.25 cup)
- Quaker Oats, rolled oats (.5 cup)
- Salt (1 pinch)
- Water or milk (1 cup)
- Cinnamon (1 pinch)
- Maple syrup or another sweetener (to your liking)
- Frozen berries of choice (1 cup)
- *Optional toppings*: Yogurt & berries

Preparation Instructions:

1. Use a jar with a lid, and add the salt, milk, seeds, oats, and cinnamon. Store in the fridge overnight.
2. Puree the berries and combine with the oats. Top it off with yogurt and more berries, honey, nuts, or other toppings of choice. Just be sure to count the added calories.

Crustless Spinach Quiche

Serving Yields: 6
Nutritional Count (each portion):
- Calories: 309
- Carbs: 4.8
- Protein: 20.4
- Total Fat: 23.7

Ingredients Needed:

- Vegetable oil (1 tbsp.)
- Onion (1 chopped)
- Frozen chopped spinach (10 oz. pkg.)
- Eggs (5 beaten)
- Shredded Muenster cheese (3 cups)
- Salt (.25 tsp.)
- Ground black pepper (.125 tsp.)
- *Also needed:* 9-inch pie pan

Preparation Instructions:

1. Lightly grease the pan. Thaw and drain the spinach.
2. Warm up the oven to reach 350° Fahrenheit.
3. Warm up the oil in a skillet using the medium-high temperature setting.
4. Toss in the onions. Sauté until they're are softened. Stir occasionally.
5. Toss the spinach into the mixture. Simmer until the excess moisture has evaporated.
6. In another container, whisk the shredded cheese with the pepper, salt, and eggs.
7. Fold in the spinach mixture, stirring well. Scoop into the pie pan.
8. Bake until the eggs are set (30 min.).
9. Cool the quiche for about 10 minutes and serve.

Deep Dish Spinach Quiche

Serving Yields: 6
Nutritional Count (each portion):
- Calories: 613
- Carbs: 23.9
- Protein: 22.9
- Total Fat: 48.2

Ingredients Needed:
- Butter (.5 cup)
- Garlic (3 chopped)
- Onion (1 small, chopped)
- Frozen chopped spinach (10 oz.)
- Mushrooms (4.5 oz.)
- Crumbled herb and garlic feta (6 oz. pkg.)
- Shredded cheddar cheese (8 oz.)
- Salt & black pepper (as desired)
- Deep dish pie crust (9-inch, unbaked)
- Eggs (4)
- Milk (1 cup)
- Black pepper & salt (to your liking)

Preparation Instructions:
1. Heat the oven to 375° Fahrenheit.
2. Thaw and drain the spinach and mushrooms.
3. Add the butter to the skillet and melt using the medium temperature heat

setting.
4. Sauté the onions and garlic for about 7 minutes until lightly browned.
5. Fold in the feta, mushrooms, spinach, .5 cup of cheese, pepper, and salt. Scoop into the pie crust.
6. Whisk the eggs and milk. Dump into the pastry shell and blend with the spinach mixture.
7. Set the timer for 15 minutes. Add the remainder of the cheddar cheese. Bake until the center is set (35 to 40 min.). Wait for approximately 10 minutes before serving.
8. Enjoy.

Delicious Scrambled Eggs

Serving Yields: 2
Nutritional Count (each portion):
- Calories: 249
- Carbs: 13
- Protein: 14
- Total Fat: 17

Ingredients Needed:
- Oil (1 tbsp.)
- Yellow pepper (1)
- Cherry tomatoes (8)
- Spring onions (2)
- Capers (1 tbsp.)
- Black olives (2 tbsp.)
- Eggs (4)

- Dried oregano (.25 tsp.)
- Black pepper (to your liking)
- *Optional for serving:* Fresh parsley

Preparation Instructions:

1. Warm up the oil in a pan using the medium temperature setting.
2. Dice the bell pepper and spring onions. Add to the skillet and sauté for a few minutes until slightly soft. Quarter the tomatoes, and slice the olives and capers. Toss into the skillet. Sauté for 1 more minute.
3. Break the eggs into the skillet and scramble.
4. Sprinkle with the black pepper and the oregano. Keep stirring until the eggs are done.
5. Serve warm, topped with a portion of fresh parsley.

Egg White Scramble With Cherry Tomatoes & Spinach

Serving Yields: 4
Nutritional Count (each portion):
- Calories: 142
- Carbs: 7
- Protein: 15
- Total Fat: 5

Ingredients Needed:
- Olive oil (1 tbsp.)
- Eggs (1 whole & 10 egg whites)
- Salt (.5 tsp.)
- Minced garlic clove (1)

- Black pepper (.25 tsp.)
- Halved cherry tomatoes (2 cups)
- Packed fresh baby spinach (2 cups)
- Light cream, half & half (.5 cup)
- Finely grated parmesan cheese (.25 cup)

Preparation Instructions:
1. Whisk the eggs, pepper, salt, and milk.
2. Prepare a skillet using the medium-high heat setting.
3. Toss in the garlic when the pan is hot. Saute for approximately 30 seconds.
4. Fold in the spinach and tomatoes. Continue sautéing for one additional minute. The tomatoes should be softened and the spinach wilted.
5. Add the egg mixture into the pan using the medium heat setting. Fold the egg gently as it cooks for about 2 to 3 minutes.
6. Remove from the burner and sprinkle with the cheese.

Eggs Baked In Tomatoes

Serving Yields: 4
Nutritional Count (each portion):
- Calories: 288
- Carbs: 12
- Protein: 18
- Total Fat: 19

Ingredients Needed:
- Olive oil (2 tbsp.)
- Large eggs (8)
- Medium tomatoes (8)
- Milk (.25 cup)

- Grated parmesan cheese (.25 cup)
- Black pepper & salt (as desired)
- Freshly chopped herbs, e.g., parsley, thyme, rosemary, or a mixture (4 tbsp.)

Preparation Instructions:

1. Warm up the oven to 375° Fahrenheit.
2. Grease a large oven-safe skillet using olive oil.
3. Prepare the tomatoes. Remove the stem and scoop out all the insides. (Reserve the pulp, and use them to make tomato sauce or salsa.)
4. Place the tomato shells in the prepared skillet.
5. Crack an egg into each of the tomatoes. Top it off with salt, pepper, and 1 tablespoon each of the milk and parmesan.
6. Bake until the tomatoes are tender, the yolks are still a little jiggly, and the egg whites are set (15 min.).
7. Let it cool for about 5 minutes. Garnish with the fresh herbs. Serve immediately.

Feta Frittata

Serving Yields: 2

Nutritional Count (each portion):
- Calories: 203
- Carbs: 7
- Protein: 17
- Total Fat: 12

Ingredients Needed:
- Green onion (1)
- Small garlic clove (1)
- Large eggs (2)
- Egg substitute (.5 cup)
- Crumbled feta cheese (Divided, 4 tbsp.)
- Plum tomato (.33 cup)
- Avocado slices (4 thin)
- Reduced-fat sour cream (2 tbsp.)
- Mozzarella cheese (1 slice)
- *Also needed*: 6-inch nonstick skillet

Preparation Instructions:
1. Peel the avocado. Thinly slice the avocado and onions. Mince the garlic, and chop the tomatoes.
2. Warm up the pan using the medium temperature setting and lightly spritz it with cooking oil.
3. Whisk the egg substitute, eggs, and 3 tablespoons of feta cheese. Empty into the skillet. Put a lid on the pan and simmer for 4 to 6 minutes.
4. Toss in the rest of the feta cheese and tomato. Place the top back on the skillet. Simmer until the eggs are set.
5. Place one slice of mozzarella on top of the prosciutto, and spread 1/4 of the avocado slices into each wrap.
6. Garnish each of the wraps with one sliced tomato and about .25 cup of lettuce leaves, torn apart.
7. Let it rest for about 5 minutes before cutting it into halves. Serve with a portion of the avocado and sour cream.

Feta-Quinoa & Egg Muffins

Serving Yields: 12

Nutritional Count (each portion):
- Calories: 114
- Carbs: 6
- Protein: 7
- Total Fat: 7

Ingredients Needed:
- Baby spinach (2 cups)
- Onion (.5 cup)
- Tomatoes, cherry or grape tomatoes work well (1 cup)
- Pitted Kalamata olives (.5 cup)
- Fresh oregano (1 tbsp.)
- High oleic sunflower oil (+) optional extra for greasing muffin tins (2 tsp.)
- Cooked quinoa (1 cup)
- Eggs (8)
- Crumbled feta cheese (1 cup)
- Salt (.25 tsp.)
- *Also needed*: 12-count silicone holders on a baking sheet/muffin tin

Preparation Instructions:
1. Warm the oven in advance to reach 350° Fahrenheit.
2. Prepare the pan with a spritz of cooking oil spray and set aside.
3. Chop the vegetables.
4. Warm up the pan using the medium heat temperature setting.
5. Pour in the oil and onions. Sauté for 2 minutes.
6. Pour in the tomatoes and sauté for one more minute.
7. Fold in the spinach and sauté until wilted (approx. 1 min.).
8. Extinguish the heat. Fold in the oregano and olives.

9. Break the eggs in a blender or mixing bowl, mixing well until combined. Combine the quinoa, feta cheese, salt, and veggie mixture. Mix all of the fixings and empty everything into the chosen pan.
10. Bake until the muffins are lightly brown (30 min.).
11. Cool the muffins on the countertop for about 5 minutes before serving or chill in the fridge. You can reheat in the microwave the next day.

French Toast Delight

Serving Yields: 12
Nutritional Count (each portion):
- Calories: 123
- Carbs: 19.4
- Protein: 4.8
- Total Fat: 2.7

Ingredients Needed:
- White sugar (1 tbsp.)
- Ground cinnamon (.5 tsp.)
- Salt (1 pinch)
- All-purpose flour (.25 cup)
- Milk (1 cup)
- Eggs (3)
- Vanilla extract (1 tsp.)
- Thick slices of bread (12)

Preparation Instructions:
1. Measure the flour and add to a mixing container. Whisk in the sugar, milk, vanilla, cinnamon, eggs, and salt.
2. Warm up a frying pan or lightly oiled griddle using the medium heat setting.

3. Soak the bread in the mixture until fully saturated.
4. Prepare each side of the french toast until lightly browned.
5. Serve hot.

Greek Omelette Casserole

Serving Yields: 12

Nutritional Count (each portion):
- Calories: 196
- Carbs: 5
- Protein: 10
- Total Fat: 12

Ingredients Needed:

- Large eggs (12)
- Whole milk (cups)
- Fresh spinach (8 oz.)
- Cloves of garlic (2 minced)
- Artichoke salad, with olives and peppers (12 oz.)
- Sun-dried tomato (.5 cup)
- Feta cheese (5 oz. crumbled)
- Dried dill (1 tsp.) or freshly chopped (1 tbsp.)
- Oregano (1 tsp.)
- Lemon pepper (1 tsp.)
- Olive oil (4 tsp., divided)
- Salt (1 tsp.)
- *Also needed*: 9x13-inch baking dish

Preparation Instructions:

1. Warm the oven to 375° Fahrenheit.
2. Chop the fresh herbs. Drain and chop the artichoke salad.
3. Add 1 tbsp of oil into a skillet using the medium heat temperature setting.
4. Sauté the garlic and spinach until wilted (3 min.).
5. Oil the baking dish and layer the spinach and artichoke salad evenly in the dish.
6. Whisk the milk, eggs, herbs, lemon pepper, and salt.
7. Empty over the vegetables and sprinkle with feta cheese.
8. Bake on the center oven rack until it's firm in the center (35-40 min.).

Herb-Sausage & Cheese Dutch Baby

Serving Yields: 4

Nutritional Count (each portion):
- Calories: 287
- Carbs: 18.9
- Protein: 13.1
- Total Fat: 17.6

Ingredients Needed:
- Bulk Italian sausage (.33 cup)
- Eggs (3 at room temperature)
- Whole milk (.66 cup at room temperature)
- All-purpose flour (.66 cup)
- Unsalted butter, divided (2 tbsp.)
- Salt (.5 tsp.)
- Black pepper (1 pinch)

- Freshly sliced chives (1 tsp.)
- Shredded white cheddar cheese (.33 cup)
- Freshly minced thyme (.5 tsp.)
- *Also needed*: 12-inch cast iron skillet & regular pan

Preparation Instructions:

1. Heat the oven to 425° Fahrenheit.
2. Place the skillet into the oven to get hot.
3. Heat another skillet using medium-high temperature setting. Toss in the sausage and sauté for 5 to 7 minutes or until browned. Discard the grease.
4. Combine the eggs, milk, salt, pepper, flour, and 1 tablespoon butter in a blender, mixing about 2 minutes until the batter is smooth and thin.
5. Carefully remove the skillet from the oven using an oven mitt, and pour the remaining 1 tablespoon of butter into the hot skillet, carefully swirling to coat. Empty the batter into the hot skillet and transfer to the oven.
6. Bake until it's puffed around the edges and cooked through (18-25 min.).
7. Mince the chives and thyme. Sprinkle the mixture with the crumbled sausage and cheese.
8. Bake until the cheese is melted (1 min.).
9. Slice and serve immediately.

Holiday Breakfast Sausage Casserole

Serving Yields: 8
Nutritional Count (each portion):
- Calories: 377
- Carbs: 13.4
- Protein: 21.5
- Total Fat: 26

Ingredients Needed:

- Ground pork sausage (1 lb.)
- Mustard powder (1 tsp.)
- Salt (.5 tsp.)
- Eggs (4)
- Milk (2 cups)
- White bread (6 slices)
- Shredded mild cheddar cheese (8 oz.)
- *Also needed*: 9x13-inch baking dish

Preparation Instructions:

1. Grease the baking pan. Warm up the oven to reach 350° Fahrenheit.
2. Toast the bread and dice into cubes.
3. Crumble the sausage into a skillet and prepare using the medium heat setting. Drain when done.
4. Whisk the eggs with the milk, salt, and mustard powder.
5. Stir in the cheese, bread cubes, and sausage.
6. Dump the fixings into the baking dish and cover with a top.
7. Store in the fridge overnight for best results or about 8 hours.
8. Bake it for 45 to 60 minutes with a lid.
9. Reduce the temperature to 325° Fahrenheit. Remove the lid and bake until set (30 min.).

Low-Carb Keto Egg & Ham Muffins

Serving Yields: 6

Nutritional Count (each portion):
- Calories: 109
- Carbs: 2
- Protein: 9
- Total Fat: 6

Ingredients Needed:
- Thin-cut deli ham (9 slices)
- Canned roasted red pepper, sliced (.5 cup+ additional for garnish)
- Fresh spinach (.33 cup, minced)
- Feta cheese (.25 cup, crumbled)
- Large eggs (5)
- Black pepper & salt (1 pinch each)
- Pesto sauce (1.5 tbsp.)
- *For the garnish*: Fresh basil

Preparation Instructions:
1. Warm the oven to reach 400° Fahrenheit. Use a spritz of cooking oil spray to prepare the muffin tin.
2. Place 1.5 pieces of ham into each cup.
3. Place a portion of roasted red peppers in the bottom of each muffin tin.
4. Place 1 tablespoon of minced spinach on top of each red pepper.
5. Top the mixture with .5 tbsp of crumbled feta cheese.
6. Whisk the salt, eggs, and pepper. Pour into the six tins.
7. Bake until the eggs are set to your liking (15 to 20 min.).
8. Remove each cup from the muffin tin.
9. Garnish with .25 tsp of the pesto sauce, more pepper slices, and freshly minced basil.

Mediterranean Omelette

Serving Yields: 1

Nutritional Count (each portion):
- Calories: 303
- Carbs: 21.9
- Protein: 18.2
- Total Fat: 17.7

Ingredients Needed:
- Butter/oil (1 tsp.)
- Eggs (2)
- Milk or cream (1 tbsp.)
- Oregano (as desired)
- Pepper & salt (as desired)
- Artichoke heart (1)
- Kalamata olives (2 tbsp.)
- Feta cheese (1 tbsp.)
- Tomato (2 tbsp.)
- Romesco sauce (1 tbsp.)

Preparation Instructions:

1. Dice the tomato and slice the olives. Quarter the artichoke.
2. Prepare a skillet with oil.
3. Whisk the egg, milk, salt, pepper, and oregano. Pour into the hot pan to simmer until the eggs have begun setting.
4. Toss in the tomatoes, olives, artichoke, and crumbled feta over half of the egg, folding the covered part over.
5. Cook the eggs until set (1 min.).
6. Take the pan from the burner and garnish with the delicious romesco sauce.

Mediterranean Toast

Serving Yields: 1

Nutritional Count (each portion):
- Calories: 333.7
- Carbs: 33.3
- Protein: 16.3
- Total Fat: 17

Ingredients Needed:
- Good whole wheat or multigrain bread (1 Slice)
- Red pepper hummus (1 tbsp.)
- Mashed avocado (.25 of 1)
- Grape/cherry tomatoes (3 sliced)
- Greek olives (3 sliced)
- Hard-boiled egg (1 sliced)
- Reduced-fat crumbled feta (1.5 tsp.)

Preparation Instructions:
1. Toast the bread, and add the hummus and mashed avocado.
2. Add the sliced cherry tomatoes and olives, followed by the sliced hard-boiled egg and feta.
3. Sprinkle to your liking with a portion of pepper and salt.

Peanut Butter & Banana Greek Yogurt Bowl

Serving Yields: 4

Nutritional Count (each portion):
- Calories: 370
- Carbs: 47.7
- Protein: 22.7
- Total Fat: 10.6

Ingredients Needed:
- Medium bananas (2)
- Flaxseed meal (.25 cup)
- Nutmeg (1 tsp.)
- Peanut butter (.25 cup)
- Vanilla Greek yogurt (4 cups)

Preparation Instructions:
1. Peel and slice the bananas. Divide the yogurt among four serving dishes. Top each one with sliced bananas.
2. Microwave the peanut butter for 30 to 40 seconds until completely melted.
3. Drizzle the peanut butter over the banana slices and sprinkle with the flaxseed meal. Dust with nutmeg and serve.

Poached Eggs

Serving Yields: 2

Nutritional Count (each portion):
- Calories: 72
- Carbs: 0.6
- Protein: 6.3
- Total Fat: 5

Ingredients Needed:
- Salt (.5 tsp.)
- Champagne vinegar (1 tsp.)
- Fresh eggs (2)

Preparation Instructions:
1. Prepare a saucepan using cold water. Boil using the medium temperature setting. Stir in the salt and vinegar.
2. Break each of the eggs into a ramekin. Place it close to the water, and slide it out of the dish. Simmer until set.
3. Use a slotted spoon to lift it from the pan to help prevent sticking. Cook until the yolk is runny and the white is cooked (6 min.).
4. Prepare a container with ice water. Take the eggs from the pan and add to the bowl of ice water. (It slows and stops the cooking process.)
5. Remove the eggs from the saucepan.
6. Drain on a layer of paper towels before serving.

Potato Hash With Poached Eggs, Chickpeas, & Asparagus

Serving Yields: 4
Nutritional Count (each portion):
- Calories: 535
- Carbs: 34.5
- Protein: 26.6
- Total Fat: 20.8

Ingredients Needed:
- Olive oil (as needed)
- Small yellow onion (1)
- Cloves of garlic (2)
- Russet potatoes (2)
- Canned chickpeas (1 cup)
- Baby asparagus (1 lb.)
- Ground allspice (1.5 tsp.)
- Za'atar (1 tsp.)
- Sweet or smoked paprika (1 tsp.)
- Coriander (1 tsp.)
- Sugar (1 pinch)
- Oregano (1 tsp.)
- Eggs (4)
- Water
- White vinegar (1 tsp.)
- Red onion (1 small)
- Roma tomatoes (2)
- Crumbled feta (.5 cup)

- Chopped fresh parsley (1 cup)
- Pepper & salt (as desired)

Preparation Instructions:

1. Chop the onions, garlic cloves, tomatoes, and potatoes. Remove the stems from the parsley. Drain and rinse the chickpeas. Cut the ends of the asparagus and chop into .25-inch pieces.
2. Warm up 1.5 tablespoons of oil into a large cast-iron skillet using the medium-high temperature setting.
3. Toss in the chopped onions, potatoes, and garlic. Sprinkle pepper and salt, to your preferred taste.
4. Simmer for 5 to 6 minutes. Stir often until the potatoes are tender.
5. Fold in the asparagus, chickpeas, and the spices, mixing well.
6. Cook for another 5 to 6 minutes. Reduce the temperature setting to low; stirring often.
7. Prepare a large pot of water, boiling to reach a steady simmer. Put 1 tsp vinegar.
8. Break the eggs in a dish. Stir the water gently and carefully slide the eggs in to simmer for exactly 3 minutes, so the egg whites will wrap around the yoke.
9. Transfer the eggs on a kitchen towel, and dust it with pepper and salt.
10. Remove the potato hash from the stove and mix with the tomatoes, feta, parsley, and chopped red onions.
11. Garnish with the poached eggs. Serve when ready.

Pumpkin Pancakes

Serving Yields: 6
Nutritional Count (each portion):
- Calories: 278
- Carbs: 45.8
- Protein: 7.9
- Total Fat: 7.2

Ingredients Needed:
- Milk (1.5 cups)
- Egg (1)
- Vegetable oil (2 tbsp.)
- Pumpkin puree (1 cup)
- Vinegar (2 tbsp.)
- Salt (.5 tsp.)
- All-purpose flour (2 cups)
- Ground allspice (1 tsp.)
- Bak. powder (2 tsp.)
- Brown sugar (3 tbsp.)
- Cinnamon (1 tsp.)
- Bak. soda (1 tsp.)
- Ground ginger (.5 tsp.)

Preparation Instructions:
1. Whisk the vinegar, oil, egg, pumpkin, and the milk together.
2. Combine the salt, ginger, cinnamon, allspice, baking soda, baking powder, brown sugar, and the flour in another mixing container.
3. Stir the fixings together just enough to combine.
4. Warm up a frying pan or oiled griddle using the medium-high temperature setting.
5. Pour the batter into the griddle. Prepare and enjoy while hot.

Quinoa Egg Breakfast Muffin

Serving Yields: 12

Nutritional Count (each portion):
- Calories: 118
- Carbs: 12
- Protein: 7
- Total Fat: 5

Ingredients Needed:
- Eggs (6)
- Black pepper & salt (.25 tsp. each)
- Cooked quinoa (1 cup)
- Mushrooms (1 cup)
- Onion (.5 of 1)
- Sun-dried tomatoes (.5 cup)
- Swiss cheese shredded (1 cup + .25 cup reserved for tops)
- *Also needed:* Standard muffin pan lined with silicone muffin liners

Preparation Instructions:
1. Warm the oven to reach 350° Fahrenheit.
2. Drain and dice the tomatoes and slice the mushrooms.
3. Beat the eggs and toss in the remainder of the fixings.
4. Spoon into the muffin tin and garnish with the rest of the cheese.
5. Test the center of the muffins for doneness. It should come out clean using a cake tester (20 to 25 min.). Serve.

Shakshuka Classic

Serving Yields: 4

Nutritional Count (each portion):
- Calories: 179
- Carbs: 12
- Protein: 7
- Total Fat: 11

Ingredients Needed:
- Olive oil (2 tbsp.)
- Onion (1)
- Red bell peppers (2)
- Garlic cloves (2)
- Chopped tomatoes (15 oz.)
- Sugar (1 tsp.)
- Spicy harissa (.5 to 1 tsp.)
- Eggs (4)
- Chopped parsley (1 tbsp.)
- Pepper & salt (as desired)

Preparation Instructions:
1. Pour oil into a heavy cast iron skillet, and wait for it to get hot.
2. Finely dice the peppers and onions and toss into the skillet. Sauté for about 5 minutes, watching closely and stirring as needed.
3. Toss in the diced garlic. Sauté for another minute.
4. Pour in the tomatoes, sugar, and harissa and continue cooking for about 7 minutes.
5. Season well with the pepper and salt; adding more harissa if you want more

spice.
6. Make four indentations in the mixture, and add an egg in each of them.
7. Cover the pot. Simmer until the egg whites are just set.
8. Top it off with fresh parsley. Serve immediately with a loaf of crusty bread.

Spanish Potato Omelet

Serving Yields: 16
Nutritional Count (each portion):
- Calories: 101
- Carbs: 5
- Protein: 6
- Total Fat: 6

Ingredients Needed:
- Russet potatoes (1 lb.)
- Olive oil (2 tbsp.)
- Medium onion (.5 cup)
- Salt (.75 tsp.)
- Ground black pepper (.25 tsp.)
- Eggs (1 dozen)
- Shredded cheddar cheese, reduced-fat (2 oz. – .5 cup)
- Medium tomato (.5 cup)
- Nonstick cooking spray
- *Also needed:* 3.5–4-quart slow cooker

Preparation Instructions:
1. Prepare the cooker with a disposable liner and spritz with a layer of cooking oil.
2. Peel and slice the potatoes into .75-inch pieces. Chop the onion and tomato.

3. Prepare a skillet with oil using the medium heat setting. Toss in the potatoes to simmer until lightly browned (5 min.). Stir often.
4. Add the chopped onion. Sauté for 2 to 3 minutes until the onion is tender. Stir often.
5. Transfer the potato mixture into the cooker. Sprinkle with pepper and salt.
6. Whisk and add the eggs on top of potato mixture. Mix slightly.
7. Place a lid on the cooker and set a timer for 2.5 hours using the low-temperature setting (or until the eggs are set).
8. Loosen the omelet with a knife and transfer the omelet to a plate. Sprinkle with cheese.
9. Place a layer of foil over the top. Let it rest for about 5 minutes to melt the cheese slightly.
10. Prepare the omelet by slicing into wedges with a garnish of tomato.
11. Serve hot or warm.

Vegan Gingerbread & Banana Quinoa Breakfast Bake

Serving Yields: 8

Nutritional Count (each portion):
- Calories: 213
- Carbs: 41
- Protein: 5
- Total Fat: 4

Ingredients Needed:
- Mashed bananas (3 cups)
- Molasses (.25 cup)
- Pure maple syrup (.25 cup)

- Cinnamon (1 tbsp.)
- Raw vanilla extract (2 tsp.)
- Ginger (1 tsp.)
- Allspice (.5 tsp.)
- Salt (.5 tsp.)
- Quinoa, uncooked (1 cup)
- Ground cloves (1 tsp.)
- Unsweetened vanilla almond milk (2.5 cups)
- Slivered almonds (.25 cup)
- *Also needed*: 2.5–3-quart casserole dish

Preparation Instructions:

1. In the casserole dish, stir the mashed banana, molasses, maple syrup, vanilla extract, cinnamon, salt, ginger, allspice, and cloves until mixed well. Stir in the quinoa.
2. Pour in the almond milk. Whisk until combined well. Cover and refrigerate overnight.
3. At breakfast, warm the oven to 350° Fahrenheit.
4. Whisk the quinoa mixture. Cover with a sheet of aluminum foil.
5. Bake until the liquid is absorbed and the quinoa mixture is set, usually 1 hr. to 1.25 hr.).
6. Switch the oven setting to high-broil and remove the foil. Sprinkle with the almonds, lightly pressed into the mixture.
7. Broil until it's golden brown (3 to 4 min.). Check often.
8. Cool for about 10 minutes.

Watermelon Feta & Balsamic Pizza

Serving Yields: 4
Nutritional Count (each portion):
- Calories: 90
- Carbs: 14
- Protein: 2
- Total Fat: 3

Ingredients Needed:
- Round watermelon (1 slice)
- Crumbled feta cheese (1 oz.)
- Kalamata olives (5 to 6, sliced)
- Mint leaves (1 tsp.)
- Balsamic glaze (.5 tbsp.)

Preparation Instructions:
1. Slice the watermelon into half at the widest part.
2. Arrange the flat side facing down on a cutting board. Slice into 1-inch thick slices from each half.
3. Slice each half into 4 wedges.
4. Place them on a round baking dish.
5. Top with olives, cheese, balsamic glaze, and mint leaves.

Chapter 3: Healthy Lunch Options

Salad Choices

Arugula Salad
Serving Yields: 4
Nutritional Count (each portion):
- Calories: 257
- Carbs: 10
- Protein: 6.2
- Total Fat: 23.2

Ingredients Needed:
- Arugula leaves (4 cups)
- Cherry tomatoes (1 cup)
- Pine nuts (.25 cup)
- Rice vinegar (1 tbsp.)
- Grapeseed or olive oil (2 tbsp.)
- Pepper & salt (as desired)
- Grated parmesan cheese (.25 cup)
- Large avocado (1 sliced)

Preparation Instructions:
1. Rinse and dry the arugula leaves, grate the cheese, and slice the cherry tomatoes into halves. Peel and slice the avocado.
2. Combine the arugula, pine nuts, tomatoes, oil, vinegar, and cheese.
3. Sprinkle with a dusting of pepper and salt as desired.
4. Cover and toss to mix. Portion onto plates with the avocado slices, and enjoy.

Chickpea Salad

Serving Yields: 4

Nutritional Count (each portion):
- Calories: 163
- Carbs: 22
- Protein: 4
- Total Fat: 7

Ingredients Needed:
- Cooked chickpeas (15 oz.)
- Roma tomato (1)
- Green medium bell pepper (.5 of 1)
- Fresh parsley (1 tbsp.)
- Small white onion (1)
- Garlic (.5 tsp.)
- Lemon (1 juiced)

Preparation Instructions:
1. Dice the green pepper, tomato, and onion. Mince the garlic.
2. Combine each of the fixings into a salad bowl and toss well.
3. Cover the salad to chill for at least 15 minutes in the fridge.
4. Serve when ready.

Cucumber Salad

Serving Yields: 4

Nutritional Calorie Count:
- Calories: 68
- Carbs: 3.4
- Protein: 1.45
- Total Fat: 5.6

Ingredients Needed:
- Cucumbers (5–6)
- Plain Greek yogurt (8 oz.)
- Garlic cloves (2)
- Oregano (1 tsp.)
- Fresh mint (1 tbsp.)
- Fine sea salt & black pepper (.125 tsp. each)

Preparation Instructions:

1. Slice the cucumbers. Mince the mint and garlic.
2. Combine the oregano, mint, garlic, and yogurt, with the cucumbers in a mixing container.
3. Sprinkle the cucumbers with black pepper and salt.
4. Chill in the refrigerator for approximately 1 hour before your meal.

Fruity Curry Chicken Salad

Serving Yields: 8

Nutritional Count (each portion):
- Calories: 229
- Carbs: 12.3
- Protein: 15.1
- Total Fat: 14

Ingredients Needed:
- Skinless, boneless chicken breast halves, cooked and diced (4)
- Celery (1 stalk)
- Green onions (4)
- Golden Delicious apple (1)
- Golden raisins (.33 cup)
- Seedless green grapes (.33 cup)
- Chopped toasted pecans (.5 cup)
- Black pepper (.125 tsp.)
- Curry powder (.5 tsp.)
- Light mayonnaise (.75 cup)

Preparation Instructions:
1. Peel, core, and dice the apple. Cut the grapes into halves and dice the rest of the veggies. Chop the pecans.
2. Combine the pecans, chicken, onions, celery, apples, grapes, raisins, curry powder, pepper, and mayonnaise.
3. Toss all of the fixings together and serve.

Honey Lime Fruit Salad

Serving Yields: 8

Nutritional Count (each portion):
- Calories: 115
- Carbs: 22.3
- Protein: 2.4
- Total Fat: 3.3

Ingredients Needed:
- Large sliced bananas (2)
- Fresh blueberries (.5 lb.)
- Fresh strawberries (1 lb.)
- Honey (2 tbsp.)
- Lime (1 juiced)
- Pine nuts (.33 cup)

Preparation Instructions:
1. Hull and slice the strawberries and bananas.
2. Toss the blueberries, bananas, and strawberries in a large salad bowl.
3. Toss with the lime juice and honey.
4. Stir well and sprinkle with the nuts before serving.

Insalata Caprese II Salad

Serving Yields: 6
Nutritional Count (each portion):
- Calories: 311
- Carbs: 6.6
- Protein: 17.9
- Total Fat: 23.9

Ingredients Needed:
- Large ripened tomato (4)
- Mozzarella cheese (1 lb.)
- Olive oil (3 tbsp.)
- Fresh basil leaves (.33 cup)
- Freshly cracked black pepper & fine sea salt (to your liking)

Preparation Instructions:
1. Slice the cheese and tomato into .25-inch thick pieces.
2. Prepare the salad by alternating and overlapping tomato slices with mozzarella cheese and basil leaves.
3. Spritz with the olive oil. Dust with a portion of the pepper and salt. Serve.

Nicoise-Style Tuna Salad With Olives & White Beans

Serving Yields: 4
Nutritional Count (each portion):
- Calories: 548
- Carbs: 33.4
- Protein: 36.3
- Total Fat: 30.3

Ingredients Needed:
- Green beans (.75 lb.)
- Solid white albacore tuna (12 oz. can)
- Great Northern beans (16 oz. can)
- Sliced black olives (2.25 oz.)
- Thinly sliced medium red onion (.25 of 1)
- Lemon juice (3 tbsp.)
- Large hard-cooked eggs (4)
- Dried oregano (1 tsp.)
- Olive oil (6 tbsp.)
- Black pepper & salt (as desired)
- Finely grated lemon zest (.5 tsp.)
- Water (.33 cup)

Preparation Instructions:
1. Drain the can of tuna, Great Northern beans, and black olives. Trim and snap the green beans into halves. Thinly slice the red onion. Cook and peel the eggs until hard boiled.
2. Add salt to the water into a pan and add the beans.
3. Place a top on the pot, and turn the temperature setting to high. Let it boil.
4. Once the beans are cooking, set a timer for 5 minutes. Immediately, drain and add the beans to a cookie sheet with a raised edge on paper towels to cool.

5. Combine the onion, olives, white beans, and drained tuna with the oil, lemon juice, zest, and oregano.
6. Dump the mixture over the salad as you gently toss.
7. Adjust the seasonings to your liking. Portion the tuna-bean salad with the green beans and eggs to serve.

Shrimp Orzo Salad

Serving Yields: 8

Nutritional Count (each portion: 1.5 cups each):
- Calories: 397
- Carbs: 52
- Protein: 18
- Total Fat: 12

Ingredients Needed:
- Orzo pasta (16 oz. pkg.)
- Cooked shrimp (.75 lb.)
- Water-packed artichoke hearts (14 oz. can)
- Sweet red pepper (1 cup)
- Red onion (.75 cup)
- Pitted greek olives (.5 cup)
- Green pepper (1 cup)
- Freshly minced parsley (.5 cup)
- Freshly chopped dill (.33 cup)
- Greek vinaigrette (.75 cup)

Preparation Instructions:
1. Peel and devein the shrimp and cook. Slice each one into thirds (31–40-

count). Finely chop the onions and peppers.
2. Make the orzo according to the package instructions. Rinse with cold water. Drain well.
3. Combine the olives, shrimp, orzo, herbs, and veggies.
4. Sprinkle with vinaigrette and toss evenly to coat.
5. Refrigerate and cover until you're ready to eat.
6. Serve as a delicious side salad.

Tomato Feta Salad

Serving Yields: 4
Nutritional Count (each portion: .75 cup each):
- Calories: 121
- Carbs: 9
- Protein: 3
- Total Fat: 9

Ingredients Needed:
- Balsamic vinegar (2 tbsp.)
- Freshly minced basil (1.5 tsp. or .5 tsp. dried)
- Salt (.5 tsp.)
- Coarsely chopped sweet onion (.5 cup)
- Olive oil (2 tbsp.)
- Cherry or grape tomatoes (1 lb.)
- Crumbled feta cheese (.25 cup.)

Preparation Instructions:
1. Whisk the salt, basil, and vinegar.
2. Toss the onion into the vinegar mixture, and let it rest for about 5 minutes
3. Slice the tomatoes into halves and stir in the tomatoes, feta cheese, and oil evenly. Serve.

Zesty Quinoa Salad
Serving Yields: 6
Nutritional Count (each portion):
- Calories: 270
- Carbs: 33.8
- Protein: 8.9
- Total Fat: 11.5

Ingredients Needed:
- Quinoa (1 cup)
- Water (2 cups)
- Limes (2 juiced)
- Olive oil (.25 cup)
- Ground cumin (2 tsp.)
- Red pepper flakes (.5 tsp. or as desired)
- Salt (1 tsp. + to taste)
- Halved cherry tomatoes (1.5 cups)
- Black beans (15 oz. can)
- Green onions (5 finely chopped)
- Freshly chopped cilantro (.25 cup)
- Ground black pepper (as desired)

Preparation Instructions:

1. Drain the black beans and rinse thoroughly. Pour water into a saucepan.
2. Once the water begins to boil, add in the quinoa. Lower the temperature setting to medium-low.
3. Put a top on the cooking pot and simmer until the water has been absorbed (10 to 15 min.). Let it cool.
4. Whisk the lime juice, oil, cumin, pepper flakes, and 1 teaspoon of salt

together in a mixing container.
5. Combine the beans, tomatoes, green onions, and quinoa together in another mixing container.
6. Pour the dressing over the prepared salad, tossing well to coat.
7. Sprinkle with the black pepper, salt, and cilantro.
8. You can serve warm or chilled in the fridge.

Zucchini, Artichoke, & Chicken Salad

Serving Yields: 6
Nutritional Count (each portion):
- Calories: 312
- Carbs: 19.5
- Protein: 15.4
- Total Fat: 20

Ingredients Needed:
- Olive oil (6 tbsp., divided)
- Zucchini (4)
- Chicken breast halves (2)
- Garbanzo beans (15 oz. can)
- Artichoke hearts (14 oz. can)
- Black olives (6 oz. can)
- Grated parmesan cheese (.5 cup)
- Black pepper & salt (to your liking)

Preparation Instructions:

1. Rinse and drain the beans, olives, and artichoke hearts and chop to bits. Cut the zucchini into 1.5-inch sticks. Remove all of the bones and skin from the breast halves and cover with black pepper and salt.
2. Warm up the pan with 2 tbsp of oil using the medium-heat setting.
3. Cook the chicken breasts until the pink is gone from the center (5 to 10 minutes on each side).
4. An internal thermometer should read at least 165° Fahrenheit (at the thickest part of the breast). Cut the chicken into .5-inch cubes and toss into a big mixing container.
5. Heat the rest of the oil using the medium heat temperature setting. Sauté and stir the zucchini with salt and pepper until slightly tender (5 min.).
6. Drain the zucchini on a paper towel-lined platter.
7. Mix the garbanzo beans, zucchini, artichoke hearts, olives, and parmesan cheese with the chicken, tossing well to combine.
8. Store in the fridge before serving (1 hr.).

Soup

Chicken Soup

Serving Yields: 4

Nutritional Count (each portion):
- Calories: 820
- Carbs: 71
- Protein: 83
- Total Fat: 24

Ingredients Needed:
- Chicken (1)
- Stock (17 cups)
- Very ripe tomatoes (8)
- Cloves of garlic (4)
- Concentrated tomato puree (.75 cup)
- Zucchini (3)
- Bell peppers (3)
- Onions (2)
- Capers (.75 cup)
- Olive oil (2 tbsp.)
- Pepper & salt (as desired)
- *For the garnish*: Chopped basil or parsley

Preparation Instructions:
1. Dice the veggies. Boil the chicken or heat the chicken stock.
2. Add tomatoes, bell peppers, and tomato puree, and let them reach the boiling and continue for 10 minutes.
3. Toss in the zucchini and capers. Bring again to boil and simmer for another 10 minutes.
4. Meanwhile, warm up another pan with oil.
5. Toss the chopped garlic and onions into the heated oil. Sauté for 5 minutes.
6. Fold in the fried onion and garlic into the soup, and let everything boil for another 10 minutes.
7. Serve and garnish to your liking.

Chickpea Garbanzo Soup

Serving Yields: 4

Nutritional Count (each portion):
- Calories: 340
- Carbs: 46
- Protein: 9
- Total Fat: 15

Ingredients Needed
- Baking soda (1 tsp.)
- Large onions (3)
- Chickpeas (3 cups)
- Black pepper (1 tbsp.)
- Freshly snipped rosemary leaves (2 tbsp.)
- Olive oil (4 tbsp.)
- Lemon (1)
- Salt (1 tbsp.)

Preparation Instructions:
1. Soak the chickpeas in a bowl the evening before you are ready to prepare, with at least twice the amount of hot water.
2. The next day, drain the chickpeas and add the bicarbonate soda. Mix well. Leave it for a while for the soda to take effect.
3. Put the chickpeas into a pot full of fresh cold water. Let it boil.
4. Chop the onions in quarters (discard the skin), and add them to the pot.
5. Remove any scum produced on top of the boiling liquid.
6. Reduce the temperature setting and cover with a lid. Simmer for at least 1 hour. Add additional boiling water as needed.

7. At the last 10 minutes of the cooking process, stir in the rosemary, salt, and pepper.
8. Mix in the olive oil and fresh lemon juice just before serving.

Creamy Italian White Bean Soup

Serving Yields: 4

Nutritional Count (each portion):
- Calories: 245
- Carbs: 38.1
- Protein: 12
- Total Fat: 4.9

Ingredients Needed:
- Onion (1)
- Celery (1 stalk)
- Garlic (1 clove)
- White kidney beans (2, 16 oz. cans)
- Chicken broth (14 oz. can)
- Vegetable oil (1 tbsp.)
- Ground black pepper (.25 tsp.)
- Dried thyme (.125 tsp.)
- Water (2 cups)
- Fresh spinach (1 bunch)
- Lemon juice (1 tbsp.)

Preparation Instructions:

1. Rinse and drain the kidney beans. Rinse and slice the spinach. Chop the onion, celery, and garlic.

2. Warm up the oil, and toss in the celery and onions. Simmer until tender (5 to 8 min.). Add the garlic and sauté for about 30 seconds. Pour in the beans, chicken broth, pepper, thyme, and water.
3. When the mixture is boiling, reduce the heat and simmer (15 min.).
4. Transfer about 2 cups of the bean and veggie mixture out of the pot.
5. In small batches, blend the remaining soup using a mixer (low-speed) until smooth. Once blended, add the soup back into the stockpot, and stir in the reserved beans.
6. Resume boiling and stir in the spinach. Simmer for 1 minute or until spinach is wilted. Pour in freshly squeezed lemon juice. Extinguish the heat and place on the countertop to cool slightly.
7. Serve with freshly grated parmesan.

Fast Seafood Gumbo

Serving Yields: 5

Nutritional Count (each portion):
- Calories: 363
- Carbs: 18
- Protein: 40
- Total Fat: 2

Ingredients Needed:
- Olive oil (.25 cup.)
- Gluten-free flour, e.g., rice, tapioca, or gluten-free blend (.25 cup.)
- Medium white onion (1)
- Celery (1 cup)
- Red & Green bell pepper (1 each)
- Red chili (1)
- Okra (fresh or frozen (2 cups)
- Canned crushed tomatoes (1 cup)

- Large cloves of garlic (2 crushed)
- Dried thyme (1 tsp.)
- Fish stock (2 cups)
- Bay leaf (1)
- Cayenne powder (1 tsp.)
- Boneless crab meat with brine (2, 8 oz. can)
- Shrimp (1 lb.)
- Salt & pepper (as desired)
- Fresh parsley (.25 cup.)

Preparation Instructions:

1. Deseed and chop the peppers, onion, red chili, okra, and garlic. Finely chop the parsley. Peel and devein the shrimp.
2. In an 8-quart stockpot, warm the oil using the medium heat setting.
3. Toss in the flour. Stir well with the oil to form a thick paste. Stir for about 5 minutes, making sure not to let the paste burn.
4. Toss in the onions, celery, peppers, and okra. Simmer for about 5 minutes. Toss in the garlic, thyme, stock bay leaf, tomatoes, and cayenne.
5. Stir well. Let it boil using the high heat temperature setting. Lower the temperature back to medium and simmer for approximately 15 minutes.
6. Fold in the raw shrimp and crab meat with brine and let the shrimp cook for 8 minutes until totally cooked. Add a portion of the parsley before serving.
7. Serve with rice and top with sliced green onions. Sprinkle with the pepper and salt to your liking.

Greek Lentil Soup

Serving Yields: 4

Nutritional Count (each portion):
- Calories: 357
- Carbs: 40.3
- Protein: 15.5
- Total Fat: 15.5

Ingredients Needed:
- Brown lentils (8 oz.)
- Olive oil (.25 cup or as needed)
- Minced garlic (1 tbsp.)
- Onion (1)
- Large carrot (1)
- Water (1 quart)
- Oregano (1 pinch)
- Dried rosemary (1 pinch)
- Bay leaves (2)
- Tomato paste (1 tbsp.)
- Ground black pepper & salt (as desired)
- *Optional*: Red wine vinegar (1 tsp.)

Preparation Instructions:
1. Mince the garlic and chop the onion and carrot.
2. Prep the lentils in a large soup pot. Fill with plenty of water to cover the beans by about 1 inch. Once the beans start boiling, simmer gently until tender (10 min.). Drain in a colander.
3. Warm up the oil in a skillet using the medium heat temperature setting. Toss

in the onion, carrot, and garlic. Simmer approximately 5 minutes.
4. Pour in the water, lentils, oregano, bay leaves, and rosemary. Once boiling, reduce the temperature setting to medium-low and cover. Cook for another 10 minutes.
5. Sprinkle with pepper and salt. Stir in the tomato paste.
6. Cover and simmer for approximately 30 to 40 minutes, stirring occasionally. Pour in water as needed.
7. When ready to serve, drizzle with vinegar and 1 teaspoon of olive oil.

Lemon Chicken Soup

Serving Yields: 4
Nutritional Count (each portion):
- Calories: 130
- Carbs: 8
- Protein: 12
- Total Fat: 7

Ingredients Needed:
- Onion (.5 cup)
- Carrots (.5 cup)
- Celery (.5 cup)
- Chicken breasts, skinless (1)
- Olive oil (1 tbsp.)
- Juiced lemons (2)
- Pepper & salt (.25 tsp. each)
- Low-sodium chicken broth (4 cups)
- Basil leaves (.25 cup)

Preparation Instructions:

1. Prep the chicken into bite-sized pieces. Chop the veggies.
2. Pour the oil into a large soup pot to heat using the medium-high heat setting.
3. Toss in the chicken and sear on all sides or for about 2 to 3 minutes. Transfer to a dish.
4. To the soup pot, add the celery, carrots, and onions. Cook for 4 to 5 minutes until the vegetables begin to caramelize slightly.
5. Sprinkle with the salt, pepper, and lemon juice. Stir and fold in the chicken.
6. Pour in the chicken broth. Lower the temperature setting to medium-low.
7. Simmer for approximately 25 minutes.
8. Finish it off with the basil leaves.

Quinoa Soup

Serving Yields: 4

Nutritional Count (each portion):
- Calories: 560
- Carbs: 93
- Protein: 25
- Total Fat: 11

Ingredients Needed:
- White onion (.5 of 1)
- Garlic cloves (5)
- Medium carrots (3)
- Olive oil (1 tbsp.)
- Dry red quinoa (.5 cup)
- Vegetable broth (6 cups)

- Garbanzo beans (15 oz. can)
- Lemon (1)
- Spinach (4 cups)
- *For the garnish:*
- Marinated artichokes
- Pesto and marinated artichokes

Preparation Instructions:

1. Drain and rinse the garbanzo beans.
2. Mince the garlic and onion. Peel and thinly slice the carrots into disks.
3. Using the medium heat setting, prepare a soup pot.
4. Sauté the garlic, onions, and carrots with the oil until lightly colored (5 min.).
5. Add the dry red quinoa to the pot and sauté for 30 seconds.
6. Pour in the broth and the beans into the pot.
7. Put the lid on the pot, slightly ajar to allow the steam to escape.
8. Lower the temperature setting to medium-low. Stir often until the quinoa is cooked (20 min.).
9. Extinguish the heat. Pour in the juice of one lemon.
10. Dump 1 cup of chopped spinach at the bottom of each bowl, and top with the soup.
11. Garnish each bowl with a tablespoon of basil pesto and a few marinated artichoke pieces.

Red Lentil Soup

Serving Yields: 5
Nutritional Count (each portion):
- Calories: 290
- Carbs: 33.8
- Protein: 13
- Total Fat: 3.2

Ingredients Needed:
- Olive oil (2 tbsp.)
- Red onion (1 small)
- Garlic cloves (4)
- Coriander (1 tsp.)
- Cumin (1 tbsp.)
- Dried red lentils (1.5 cups)
- Diced tomatoes (14 oz. can or 1.5 cups fresh)
- Vegetable broth (6 cups)

Preparation Instructions:
1. Warm up the oil in a large pan using a medium heat temperature setting.
2. Dice and add in the onion. Simmer, occasionally stirring, until soft and translucent (5 min.).
3. Toss in the garlic, cumin, and coriander and sauté for another minute until the garlic becomes very fragrant.
4. Stir in the lentils, broth, and tomatoes.
5. Let the liquid come to a boil. Lower the heat and simmer. Continue cooking, uncovered, until the lentils are softened (20 min.).
6. Thin the soup with a small amount of water if it becomes too thick while

cooking.
7. Pour in the lemon juice and harissa with a sprinkle of salt and pepper to your liking.
8. Serve in bowls and top with parsley and cilantro.

Vegetable Noodle Soup

Serving Yields: 4
Nutritional Count (each portion):
- Calories: 316
- Carbs: 54
- Protein: 11
- Total Fat: 5

Ingredients Needed:
- Olive oil (1 tbsp.)
- Sweet onion (1)
- Fresh tomatoes (2 cups)
- Garlic cloves (2)
- Tomato juice (2 cups)
- Red wine (.5 cup.)
- Vegetable broth (2 cups)
- Cooked chickpeas/white beans (2 cups)
- Fresh basil (3 minced tbsp.)
- Fresh sage (2 tbsp.) or dried sage (1 tsp.)
- Fresh rosemary (.5 tsp.)
- Uncooked orzo pasta or whole wheat macaroni (.5 cup.)
- Greens (2 cups)
- Hot sauce (2–3 drops)
- Salt & pepper (as desired)

Preparation Instructions:

1. Finely chop the greens, sage, onions, and rosemary. Mince the garlic and tomatoes.
2. Prepare a saucepan with the oil using the medium-low temperature setting. Sauté the garlic for 5 to 7 minutes.
3. Pour in the tomato juice, wine, and tomatoes. Simmer for approximately 20 to 30 minutes.
4. Empty the cooked white beans, vegetable broth, sage, basil, and rosemary. Raise the temperature setting to medium-high.
5. Once the soup has started to boil, dump in the uncooked pasta.
6. Lower the temperature setting, and simmer (7 min. is ideal).
7. Fold in the greens and simmer until the greens are soft and lightly cooked and the pasta is cooked the way you like it (5 min.).
8. Sprinkle in the hot sauce, salt, and pepper.
9. *Note*: Use greens that cook quicker, such as spinach, chard, or beet. Use low-sodium broth if possible.

Other Delicious Options

Fasolakia - Green Beans & Potatoes

Serving Yields: 4
Nutritional Count (each portion):
- Calories: 289
- Carbs: 38.6
- Protein: 6.8
- Total Fat: 14.1

Ingredients Needed:
- Olive oil (.25 cup)
- Small onion (1 grated)
- Fresh green beans (1.5 lb.)
- Tomatoes (4 pureed)
- Yellow potatoes (2)
- *Optional*: White sugar (1 pinch)
- Salt (.5 tsp.)
- Black pepper (as desired)
- Water (to cover)

Preparation Instructions:
1. Grate the onion and trim the green beans. Peel and slice the potatoes into wedges.
2. Warm up the olive oil in a pan using the medium temperature setting. Stir in the onion. Sauté to soften the onion (5 min.).
3. Toss in the green beans and stir to coat in the oil.
4. Simmer while occasionally stirring (2 to 3 min.). Add the pureed tomatoes, potatoes, salt, pepper, and sugar. Stir well then add water until beans are barely covered.
5. Simmer, partially covered with a lid, using the medium-low heat until potatoes and beans are softened (25 to 30 min.).
6. Uncover toward the end of cooking to reduce the sauce if it is too watery.

Fried Rice With Spinach, Peppers, & Artichokes

Serving Yields: 4

Nutritional Count (each portion):
- Calories: 244
- Carbs: 26.2
- Protein: 9.3
- Total Fat: 12.9

Ingredients Needed:
- Cooked rice (1.5 cups)
- Frozen spinach (10 oz.)
- Marinated artichoke hearts (6 oz.)
- Roasted red peppers (4 oz.)
- Minced garlic (.5 tsp.)
- Crumbled feta cheese with herbs (.5 cup)
- Olive oil (2 tbsp.)

Preparation Instructions:
1. Prepare the vegetables. Mince the garlic. Thaw, drain, and chop the frozen spinach. Drain and quarter the artichoke hearts. Drain and chop the roasted red peppers.
2. Use the medium temperature setting on the stovetop to warm up a skillet. Pour in the oil. Toss in the garlic to cook for 2 minutes.
3. Toss in the rice and simmer about 2 minutes until well heated.
4. Fold in the spinach and continue cooking for three more minutes.
5. Toss in the red peppers and artichoke hearts. Simmer for 2 minutes.
6. Stir in the feta cheese and serve immediately.

Hummus & Prosciutto Wraps

Serving Yields: 4

Nutritional Count (each portion):
- Calories: 345
- Carbs: 24
- Protein: 20
- Total Fat: 23.4

Ingredients Needed:
- Thinly sliced prosciutto (12)
- Whole wheat tortillas, low-carb (4–10-inch)
- Hummus spread (.5 cup, divided)
- Mozzarella cheese (4 slices)
- Avocado (1)
- Small tomatoes (4)
- Torn lettuce leaves (1 cup, divided)

Preparation Instructions:
1. Peel, remove the pit from the avocado, and slice it, along with the tomatoes.
2. Warm up the oven to reach 350° Fahrenheit.
3. Set up a baking tin with a layer of parchment baking paper, and add the slices of prosciutto, so they don't touch.
4. Bake for 6 to 8 minutes. Transfer the pan to the countertop to cool.
5. Stack the tortillas on a platter. Set the microwave using the high-temperature setting until hot (20 to 30 seconds).
6. Spread 2 tbsp of hummus spread and three slices of crisped prosciutto onto each of the wraps.
7. Add one slice of cheese and avocado slices on top of each wrap, along

with a slice of tomato and torn lettuce leaves.
8. Fold in at the bottom of each one (up about 2 inches). Roll and gently wrap each one to serve.

Linguine With Garlicky Clams & Peas

Serving Yields: 4

Nutritional Count (each portion):
- Calories: 368
- Carbs: 46.5
- Protein: 19.8
- Total Fat: 11.9

Ingredients Needed:
- Fresh linguine (9 oz. pkg.)
- Bottled garlic (1.5 tsp.)
- Olive oil (2 tbsp.)
- Chopped clams, undrained (3, 6.5 oz. can)
- Dry white wine (.25 cup)
- Organic vegetable broth (1 cup)
- Crushed red pepper (.25 tsp.)
- Frozen green peas (1 cup)
- Freshly chopped basil (2 tbsp.)
- Shredded parmesan cheese (.5 cup or 2 oz.)

Preparation Instructions:

1. Prepare the pasta according to the package instructions. Omit the fat and salt. Drain and cover to help keep it warm.
2. Warm the oil in a frying pan using the medium-high temperature setting.

Mince and toss the garlic into the pan. Sauté for about 1 minute.
3. Drain the clams (reserving .5 cup of the liquids).
4. Add the wine, reserved clam juice, broth, and pepper into the pan.
5. When it starts to boil, lower the temperature setting. Simmer for 5 minutes. Mix occasionally.
6. Pour the peas and clams into the pan. Simmer until thoroughly heated (2 min.). Add the pasta, tossing well.
7. Garnish the linguine mixture with the basil and cheese.

Quinoa Black Bean Burger

Serving Yields: 5

Nutritional Count (each portion):
- Calories: 245
- Carbs: 28.9
- Protein: 9.3
- Total Fat: 10.6

Ingredients Needed:
- Black beans (15 oz. can)
- Quinoa (.25 cup)
- Water (.5 cup)
- Breadcrumbs (.5 cup)
- Yellow bell pepper (.25 cup)
- Onion (2 tbsp.)
- Large clove of garlic (1)
- Cumin (1.5 tsp.)
- Salt (.5 tsp.)

- Hot pepper sauce (1 tsp.)
- Egg (1)
- Olive oil (3 tbsp.)

Preparation Instructions:

1. Mince the garlic, onion, and bell pepper. Rinse the beans and drain.
2. Add water to a saucepan. After it boils, toss in the quinoa. Let it come to a boil again, and reduce the temperature setting to medium-low. Place a lid on the pan and simmer until the water has been absorbed (15 to 20 min.).
3. Use a fork to smash the beans into a paste-like mixture, leaving some whole black beans.
4. With your hands, mix the garlic, quinoa, breadcrumbs, salt, onion, bell pepper, cumin, egg, and hot pepper sauce into mashed the black beans, shaping them into five patties.
5. Pour oil into a skillet. When it's hot, fry the patties until heated through (2 to 3 min. per side).

Skillet Gnocchi With White Beans & Chard

Serving Yields: 6

Nutritional Count (each portion):
- Calories: 259
- Carbs: 29.5
- Protein: 9.7
- Total Fat: 11.1

Ingredients Needed:
- Extra-virgin olive oil (1 tbsp.)
- Shelf-stable gnocchi (16 oz. pkg.)

- White beans (15 oz. can)
- Extra-virgin olive oil (1 tsp.)
- Yellow onion (1 medium)
- Garlic cloves (4)
- Water (.5 cup)
- Chard leaves/spinach (6 cups)
- Diced tomatoes & Italian seasonings (15 oz. can)
- Freshly ground pepper (.25 tsp.)
- Part-skim mozzarella cheese (.5 cup)
- Parmesan cheese (.25 cup)

Preparation Instructions:

1. Mince the garlic and thinly slice the onions. Chop the spinach/chard leaves, and rinse the white beans. Finely shred the mozzarella and parmesan cheese.
2. Warm up the oil in a pan using the medium temperature setting. Pour in the gnocchi and simmer until it starts to brown (5 to 7 min.). Pour into a bowl.
3. Add the remainder of the oil and toss in the onion. Sauté the fixings in a skillet using medium heat for 2 minutes. Pour in the water and garlic. Cover and simmer until the onion is softened (4 to 6 min.).
4. Fold in the chard and simmer until it wilts (1 to 2 min.).
5. Pour in the tomatoes, beans, and black pepper. Simmer and stir in the gnocchi, a sprinkle of mozzarella, and parmesan.
6. Cover and simmer until the cheese is melted (approx. 3 min.).

Sweet Slaw

Serving Yields: 8

Nutritional Count (each portion):
- Calories: 200
- Carbs: 22.5
- Protein: 0.8
- Total Fat: 12

Ingredients Needed:
- Diced onion (2 tbsp.)
- Creamy salad dressing (.66 cup)
- Vegetable oil (3 tbsp.)
- White sugar (.5 cup)
- White vinegar (1 tbsp.)
- Salt (.25 tsp.)
- Poppy seeds (.5 tsp.)
- Coleslaw mix 16 oz. bag)

Preparation Instructions:
1. Dice the onion with the coleslaw large mixing container.
2. Whisk the vegetable oil, sugar, vinegar, salt and poppy seeds in a mixing container.
3. Combine everything, tossing well.
4. Store in the refrigerator to chill for about 2 hours before mealtime.

Chapter 4: Favorite Dinner Choices

Poultry Options

Chicken & Orzo Pasta

Serving Yields: 4
Nutritional Count (each portion):
- Calories: 462
- Carbs: 52.3
- Protein: 18
- Total Fat: 19.9

Ingredients Needed:
- Uncooked orzo pasta (.5 lb.)
- Olive oil (.25 cup)
- Red wine vinegar (.33 cup)
- Dijon mustard (1 tsp.)
- Garlic powder (.75 tsp.)
- Oregano (.75 tsp.)
- Dried basil (.75 tsp.)
- Onion powder (.75 tsp.)
- Salt (.5 tsp.)
- Freshly cracked black pepper (.25 tsp.)
- Grape tomatoes (.5 cup)
- Black olives (.25 cup)
- Feta cheese (2 oz.)
- Grilled chicken breast (1)
- Red bell peppers (2)

- Sprigs fresh oregano (4)

Preparation Instructions:

1. Dice the chicken. Prepare the veggies. Slice the tomatoes into halves, and dice the peppers and olives.
2. Prepare a pot using the high-heat temperature setting. When the water starts to boil, stir in the orzo.
3. Simmer uncovered until the pasta is al dente (11 min.).
4. Drain well in a colander, pour into a container, and let cool in the fridge.
5. Whisk the vinegar, mustard, salt, olive oil, basil, garlic powder, black pepper, oregano, and onion powder.
6. In another mixing container, mix the cooked orzo, crumbled feta cheese, olives, tomatoes, and breast meat until fully incorporated.
7. Dump the dressing over the mixture, tossing well. Spoon into the red pepper halves with a portion of the fresh oregano sprigs.

Chicken Breast Cutlets With Capers & Artichokes

Serving Yields: 6

Nutritional Count (each portion):
- Calories: 408
- Carbs: 22
- Protein: 40.1
- Total Fat: 18.6

Ingredients Needed:
- White or whole wheat flour (1 cup)
- Salt (.5 tsp.)
- White pepper (.125 tsp.)

- Black pepper (.125 tsp.)
- Chicken breast strips/tenderloin (2 lb.)
- Canola & Olive oil (2 tbsp. each)
- Chicken broth (2 cups)
- Quartered marinated artichoke hearts, with liquid (12. oz. jar)
- Capers (.25 cup)
- Butter (2 tbsp.)
- Chopped flat-leaf parsley (.25 cup)
- Lemon juice (2 tbsp.)

Preparation Instructions:

1. Squeeze the lemon for the juice. Whisk the salt, flour, white pepper, and black pepper. Roll the chicken into the flour while you shake off the extra.
2. Warm up both types of oil into a skillet using the medium-high temperature setting.
3. Cook the chicken until it is well done.
4. Pour in the juice and chicken broth. Simmer as you scrape the bottom to remove the caramelized bits.
5. Quarter and add capers and artichoke hearts. Simmer until the volume is reduced by approximately half.
6. Stir the butter to melt, and toss the prepared chicken back into the pan.
7. Simmer and add in the sauce to reheat. Chop the parsley and sprinkle over the dish before serving.

Chicken Sausage Gnocchi Skillet

Serving Yields: 4
Nutritional Count (each portion):
- Calories: 430
- Carbs: 11.7
- Protein: 15.3
- Total Fat: 36.1

Ingredients Needed:
- Ricotta cheese gnocchi (8 oz.)
- Broccoli florets (2 cups)
- Butter (1 tsp.)
- Diced onion (2 tbsp., divided)
- Minced garlic (1 tbsp., divided)
- Chicken sausage links (2)
- Butter (.5 cup)
- All-purpose flour (2 tsp.)
- Black pepper & salt (as desired)

Preparation Instructions:
1. Prepare a large pot of water. Add a shake of salt to the water. Once boiling, add the gnocchi and simmer for 2 to 4 minutes. Pour in a colander to drain.
2. Arrange a steamer insert into a saucepan with just enough water to reach the base of the steamer.
3. After it starts to boil, add the broccoli. Place a lid on the pot and steam until tender (4 to 5 min.). Drain and keep warm.
4. Next, add the butter to a skillet using the medium-heat temperature setting.
5. Toss in 1 tablespoon of onion and 1 teaspoon garlic. Simmer until fragrant or about 2 minutes. Fold in the sausage, cooking until browned (5 min.).

Fold in the broccoli.
6. Melt .5 cup butter in another skillet and add the rest of the onion, garlic, and flour.
7. Continue cooking until golden brown (2 to 3 min.). Stir in the gnocchi.
8. Combine everything, mixing well before serving.

Feta Chicken Burgers

Serving Yields: 6

Nutritional Count (each portion):
- Calories: 356 with 1 tbsp. sauce
- Carbs: 25
- Protein: 31
- Total Fat: 14

Ingredients Needed:
- Reduced-fat mayonnaise (.25 cup)
- Finely chopped cucumber (.25 cup)
- Black pepper (.25 tsp.)
- Garlic powder (1 tsp.)
- Chopped roasted sweet red pepper (.5 cup)
- Greek seasoning (.5 tsp.)
- Lean ground chicken (1.5 lb.)
- Crumbled feta cheese (1 cup)
- Whole wheat burger buns (6 toasted)

Preparation Instructions:
1. Warm up the broiler to the oven ahead of time. Combine the mayonnaise and cucumber. Set aside.
2. Combine all of the seasonings and the red pepper for the burgers. Work in

the chicken and the cheese. Shape into six ½-inch thick patties.
3. Broil the burgers approximately 4 inches from the heat source. It should take about 3 to 4 minutes per side until the thermometer reaches 165° Fahrenheit.
4. Serve on the buns with the cucumber sauce. Top it off with tomato and lettuce if desired and serve.

Grecian Pasta Chicken Skillet

Serving Yields: 4, 1.5 cups each:
Nutritional Count (each portion):
- Calories: 373
- Carbs: 30
- Protein: 25
- Total Fat: 15

Ingredients Needed:
- Olive oil (1 tbsp.)
- Reduced-sodium chicken broth (14.5 oz. can)
- Undrained diced tomatoes, no salt added (14.5 oz. can)
- Chicken breast, cut into 1-inch pieces (.75 lb.)
- Water or white wine (.5 cup)
- Garlic (1 clove)
- Chopped green onion (1)
- Dried oregano (.5 tsp.)
- Multigrain thin spaghetti (4 oz.)
- Marinated and quartered artichoke hearts (7.5 oz. jar)
- Roasted sweet bell pepper strips (.25 cup)
- Sliced ripe olives (.25 cup)
- Baby spinach (2 cups)

- Lemon juice (2 tbsp.)
- Lemon zest (.5 tsp.)
- Pepper (.5 tsp.)
- Fresh parsley (2 tbsp.)
- *Optional:* Reduced-fat feta cheese (to your liking)

Preparation Instructions:
1. Drain and coarsely chop the artichoke hearts. Grate the lemon for the zest.
2. Combine the water/wine, chicken, garlic, oregano, chicken broth, and tomatoes in a large skillet.
3. Toss in the spaghetti and boil for 5 to 7 minutes. Simmer until the pink is removed from the chicken.
4. Stir in the spinach, pepper, oil, parsley, green onion, olives, red peppers, and the juice and zest of lemon.
5. Simmer until the spinach is wilted (2 to 3 min.).
6. Sprinkle with the crumbled cheese and serve.

Italian Chicken Skillet
Serving Yields: 4
Nutritional Count (each portion):
- Calories: 515
- Carbs: 53.7
- Protein: 42.5
- Total Fat: 12.9

Ingredients Needed:
- Olive oil (1 tbsp.)
- Chicken breast halves (4)
- Garlic (2 cloves)

- Red cooking wine (.5 cup)
- Italian style diced tomatoes (28 oz. can)
- Seashell pasta (8 oz.)
- Freshly chopped spinach (5 oz.)
- Shredded mozzarella cheese (1 cup)

Preparation Instructions:

1. Warm up a large skillet, and add the oil.
2. Slice the chicken into halves and simmer for approximately 5 to 8 minutes.
3. Pour in the diced tomatoes and wine. Let it come to a boil using the high-heat temperature setting.
4. Stir in the pasta. Leave the top off and continue cooking. Stir occasionally until the shells are thoroughly cooked (10 min. after the pasta starts boiling).
5. Toss in the spinach over the pasta. Place a lid on the pot to simmer for about 5 minutes.
6. Lastly, dust it with the cheese. Simmer for another 5 minutes or until the cheese bubbles.

Lemon Chicken Piccata

Serving Yields: 4

Nutritional Count (each portion):
- Calories: 421
- Carbs: 16.1
- Protein: 41.1
- Total Fat: 21.2

Ingredients Needed:

- Chicken breast halves (3)
- Butter (3 tbsp.)

- Black pepper & salt (as desired)
- All-purpose flour (.5 cup)
- Vegetable oil (2 tbsp.)
- Lemon (.5 of 1)
- Fresh lemon juice (.25 cup)
- Chicken broth low-sodium(1 cup)
- Garlic (1 minced clove)
- Capers (2 tbsp.)
- Flat-leaf Italian parsley (2 tbsp.)

Preparation Instructions:

1. Drain and rinse the capers. Mince the clove and parsley. Thinly slice the lemon.
2. Warm up the oven to 20o° Fahrenheit. Also, warm up a serving platter in the oven.
3. Remove all of the bones and visible skin from the chicken breasts. Slice into .5-inch medallions. Sprinkle with pepper and salt. Coat the chicken in the flour. Shake away the excess.
4. Warm up the oil in a skillet. Simmer for about 3 minutes on each side, working in batches. Add oil as needed.
5. Keep the prepared chicken warm in the oven. Drain most of the oil from the skillet.
6. Add and sauté the minced garlic until fragrant (20 sec.). Pour in the chicken broth, scraping the browned bits from the bottom of the skillet.
7. Toss the lemon slices into the skillet. Stir and simmer until the sauce reduces to about two-thirds of a cup (5 to 8 min.).
8. Pour in the capers and lemon juice. Continue to simmer until the sauce is slightly thickened (5 min.).
9. Add the butter into the skillet to combine with the sauce. Sprinkle in the parsley and remove from the hot burner.
10. Place the chicken medallions onto serving plates with a portion of sauce.

Lemon Chicken Skewers

Serving Yields: 6

Nutritional Count (each portion):
- Calories: 219
- Carbs: 12
- Protein: 29
- Total Fat: 6

Ingredients Needed:
- Lemon juice (3 tbsp.)
- White wine vinegar (1 tbsp.)
- Olive oil (.25 cup)
- Lemon zest (2 tsp.)
- Salt (1 tsp.)
- Dried oregano (.25 tsp.)
- Sugar (.5 tsp.)
- Black pepper (.25 tsp.)
- Zucchini (3 medium, 1.5-inch slices)
- Minced garlic (2 cloves)
- Medium onions (3 into wedges)
- Cherry tomatoes (12)
- Chicken breasts (1.5 lb.)

Preparation Instructions:

1. Cut the zucchini in half, lengthwise, and slice into 1.5-inch slices.
2. Peel the onions and cut into wedges. Zest the lemon. Cut the chicken into 1.5-inch pieces.
3. Prepare the marinade; combine the sugar, pepper, oregano, salt, lemon zest, vinegar, lemon juice, and oil, reserving .25 cup for basting.

4. Fold in the chicken and toss to cover.
5. Add the rest of the marinade in a mixing container and add the tomatoes, onions, and zucchini. Store in the fridge overnight (covered for best results) or a minimum of 4 hours.
6. When ready to cook, drain the marinade and throw away.
7. Soak the wooden skewers in water.
8. Thread the chicken and veggies onto the soaked skewers.
9. Arrange the skewers on the grill for 6 minutes using the medium heat setting. It's done when poked with a fork; the juices will run clear.

Quick Chicken Marsala

Serving Yields: 4
Nutritional Count (each portion):
- Calories: 344
- Carbs: 9
- Protein: 28
- Total Fat: 17

Ingredients Needed:
- Olive oil (2 tbsp., divided)
- Skinless, boneless chicken breast cutlets 4 (4, 4 oz.)
- Black pepper (.75 tsp. divided)
- Kosher salt (.5 tsp., divided)
- Pre-sliced button mushrooms (1, 8-oz. pkg.)
- Thyme sprigs (4)
- All-purpose flour (1 tbsp.)
- Unsalted chicken stock (.66 cup)
- Marsala wine (.66 cup)
- Unsalted butter (2.5 tbsp.)
- *Optional:* Chopped fresh thyme (1 tbsp.)

Preparation Instructions:

1. Warm up 1 tablespoon of olive oil in a skillet using medium-high temperature.
2. Discard the bones and skin from the chicken and sprinkle the chicken with 0.5 teaspoon pepper and half of the salt.
3. Toss the chicken to the hot pan and fry until done (4 min. per side).
4. Transfer the chicken from the skillet.
5. Add the remainder of the oil to the pan. Toss in the mushrooms and thyme sprigs. Simmer until the mushrooms are browned (6 min.).
6. Sprinkle in the flour and stir for 2 minutes.
7. Mix in the wine and stock. Bring to a boil, and cook until slightly thickened (2 to 3 min.).
8. Transfer the pan from the heat. Stir in the butter, the rest of the pepper, and salt.
9. Toss the chicken back into the skillet, turning to coat.
10. Discard thyme sprigs before serving. Sprinkle with chopped thyme, if desired.

Sicilian Olive Chicken

Serving Yields: 4

Nutritional Count (each portion):
- Calories: 207
- Carbs: 7.8
- Protein: 29.5
- Total Fat: 6.8

Ingredients Needed:
- Diced tomatoes (14 oz. can)
- Frozen spinach (1.5 cups)
- Halved olives (.33 cup)
- Capers (1 tbsp.)
- Crushed red pepper (.25 tsp.)
- Chicken cutlets (4, 4 ounces)
- Black pepper (1 tbsp.)
- Olive oil (1 tbsp.)

Preparation Instructions:
1. Rinse the capers and mix in with the tomatoes, olives, spinach (thawed and chopped), salt, pepper, and crushed red pepper in a mixing container.
2. Warm up the oil in a skillet using the medium-high heat setting. Cook the chicken until lightly browned for 2 to 4 minutes (side one).
3. Flip it and combine with the tomato mixture. Lower the temperature to medium. Place a lid on the skillet and simmer until fully cooked or about 3 to 5 minutes.
4. *Note:* You can use diced tomatoes with olive oil, garlic, or other tasty Italian-style seasonings.

Slow-Cooked Lemon Chicken

Serving Yields: 6

Nutritional Count (each portion):
- Calories: 336
- Carbs: 1
- Protein: 56
- Total Fat: 10

Ingredients Needed:
- Bone-in chicken breast halves (6, 12 oz. each)
- Dried oregano (1 tsp.)
- Seasoned salt (.5 tsp.)
- Pepper (.25 tsp.)
- Butter (2 tbsp.)
- Water (.25 cup)
- Fresh parsley (2 tsp.)
- Minced garlic (2 cloves)
- Lemon juice (3 tbsp.)
- Chicken bouillon granules (1 tsp.)
- *Optional*: Cooked hot rice
- *Also needed*: 5-quart slow cooker & skillet

Preparation Instructions:
1. Remove the skin from chicken. Pat it dry with paper towels.
2. Combine the pepper, seasoned salt, and oregano; rub this over the chicken.
3. Prepare a skillet using the medium-heat setting. Add the butter.
4. Brown the chicken. Transfer into the cooker.
5. Pour the water over the chicken.
6. Secure the lid and set on the low setting for 5 to 6 hours.
7. Continue to baste the chicken as it cooks with the cooking juices. Add the minced parsley. Place the lid on the pot and cook for 15 to 30 minutes longer.
8. Serve with a portion of rice if desired.

Slow Cooked Mediterranean Roasted Turkey Breast

Serving Yields: 8

Nutritional Count (each portion):
- Calories: 333
- Carbs: 8.9
- Protein: 60.6
- Total Fat: 4.7

Ingredients Needed:
- Chicken broth (Divided, .5 cup)
- Boneless turkey breast (4 lb.)
- Fresh lemon juice (2 tbsp.)
- Chopped onion (2 cups)
- Pitted Kalamata olives (.5 cup)
- Oil-packed sun-dried tomatoes (.5 cup)
- Greek seasoning, such as McCormick's (1 tsp.)
- Black pepper (.25 tsp.)
- Salt (.5 tsp.)
- All-purpose flour (3 tbsp.)

Preparation Instructions:
1. Trim the turkey and toss into the cooker with the salt, Greek seasoning, thinly sliced tomatoes, onions, lemon juice, olives, and .25 cup of the chicken broth.
2. Secure the lid, and set the timer for 7 hours on the low setting.
3. Combine the rest of the broth with the flour in a small mixing container. Whisk until smooth, and stir into the slow cooker at the end of the 7-hour cooking time.
4. Place a lid on the cooker pot. Continue cooking on low for another 30 minutes before serving.

Super Tender Chicken

Serving Yields: 4

Nutritional Count (each portion):
- Calories: 420
- Carbs: 16
- Protein: 30
- Total Fat: 26

Ingredients Needed:
- Skinless/boneless breasts of chicken (4)
- Greek yogurt (1 cup)
- Parmesan cheese (.5 cup)
- Garlic powder (1 tsp.)
- Black pepper (.5 tsp.)
- Seasoning salt (1 tsp.)

Preparation Instructions:
1. Warm up the oven ahead of time by 375° Fahrenheit.
2. Combine the mayonnaise, parmesan cheese, seasoning salt, black pepper, and garlic powder.
3. Spread the mixture evenly on top of the chicken breasts.
4. Put the chicken into a baking dish. Bake until thoroughly cooked (45 min.).
5. Transfer to the countertop and serve.

Seafood

Avocado & Tuna Tapas

Serving Yields: 4
Nutritional Count (each portion):
- Calories: 294
- Carbs: 11
- Protein: 23.9
- Total Fat: 18.2

Ingredients Needed:
- Solid white tuna, water-packed (12 oz. can)
- Mayonnaise (1 tbsp.)
- Green onions (3 + more for garnish)
- Red bell pepper (.5 of 1)
- Garlic salt and black pepper (to your liking)
- Balsamic vinegar (1 dash)
- Ripe avocados (2)

Preparation Instructions:
1. Drain the tuna well. Chop the bell pepper, and thinly slice the onions. Remove the pit of the avocados and slice in halves.
2. Whisk the vinegar, red pepper, onions, mayonnaise, and tuna.
3. Sprinkle with the black pepper and salt.
4. Load the avocado halves with the tuna.
5. Top it off with a portion of green onions and black pepper. Serve.

Baked Salmon With Dill

Serving Yields: 4
Nutritional Count (each portion: 1 fillet & 1 lemon wedge):
- Calories: 251
- Carbs: 1
- Protein: 34
- Total Fat: 12

Ingredients Needed:
- Salmon fillets (4, 6 oz. portions, 1-inch thick)
- Fresh dill (1.5 tbsp.)
- Black pepper (.125 tsp.)
- Kosher salt (.5 tsp.)
- Lemon wedges (4)

Preparation Instructions:
1. Warm up the oven to reach 350° Fahrenheit.
2. Grease a baking tin with a spritz of cooking oil spray, and add the fish.
3. Lightly spritz the fish with the spray, along with a shake of salt, pepper, and finely chopped dill.
4. Bake for 10 minutes. The fish is easily flaked with a fork when it's ready.
5. Serve with lemon wedges.

Feta Shrimp Skillet

Serving Yields: 4
Nutritional Count (each portion):
- Calories: 240
- Carbs: 16
- Protein: 25
- Total Fat: 8

Ingredients Needed:
- Olive oil (1 tbsp.)
- Garlic cloves (3)
- Onion (1 medium)
- Dried oregano (1 tsp.)
- Pepper (.5 tsp.)
- Salt (.25 tsp.)
- Undrained diced tomatoes (2 cans, 14.5 oz. each)
- *Optional:* White wine (.25 cup)
- Uncooked medium shrimp (1 lb.)
- Minced fresh parsley (2 tbsp.)
- Crumbled feta cheese (.75 cup)

Preparation Instructions:
1. Finely chop the onion. Mince the garlic. Peel and devein the shrimp.
2. Warm up the oil in a skillet using the medium-high heat setting. Toss the onion into the pan to sauté until tender (4 to 6 min.).

3. Add the garlic and seasonings. Empty the tomatoes and wine. Boil, lower the heat and remove the lid.
4. Simmer for another 5 to 7 minutes or until sauce is slightly thickened.
5. Shake in the parsley and add the shrimp. Simmer the mixture until the shrimp turns pink (5 to 6 min.) Stir occasionally.
6. Take the pan from heat and sprinkle with cheese.
7. Let it stand, covered for several minutes until the cheese is softened.

Flounder - Mediterranean Style

Serving Yields: 4
Nutritional Count (each portion):
- Calories: 282
- Carbs: 8.2
- Protein: 24.4
- Total Fat: 15.4

Ingredients Needed:
- Plum/Roma tomatoes (5)
- Extra-virgin olive oil (2 tbsp.)
- Spanish onion (.5 of 1)
- Garlic (2 cloves)
- Italian seasoning (1 pinch)
- Kalamata olives (24)
- White wine (.25 cup)
- Capers (.25 cup)
- Lemon juice (1 tsp.)
- Basil (6 sprigs)
- Parmesan cheese (3 tbsp.)
- Flounder fillets (1 lb.)

- Fresh basil (6 torn leaves)

Preparation Instructions:

1. Remove the pit from the olives and chop. Chop the garlic and onion. Grate the parmesan.
2. Warm up the oven to reach 425° Fahrenheit.
3. Prepare a pan of water. Wait for it to boil.
4. Toss in the tomatoes and quickly transfer to a bowl of ice water to stop the cooking process. You only want to blister the skins.
5. Drain and remove the skins and dice. Place it to the side for now.
6. Heat up a skillet, and add some oil in medium-heat setting. Sauté the onions until tender (5 min.).
7. Stir in the tomatoes, garlic, and Italian seasoning.
8. Simmer for about 5 to 7 minutes or until the tomatoes are tender. Stir in the lemon juice, olives, wine, capers, and half of the basil.
9. Lower the heat, and blend in the parmesan cheese. Simmer for about 15 minutes or until it's a thick sauce.
10. Arrange the flounder in a baking dish. Dump the prepared sauce over the fillets and garnish with the rest of the basil leaves.
11. Set a timer for 12 minutes. It is ready when the fish is easily flaked using a fork.

Halibut & Capers
Serving Yields: 4
Nutritional Count (each portion):
- Calories: 284
- Carbs: 1.4
- Protein: 24.2
- Total Fat: 17

Ingredients Needed:
- Olive oil (1 tbsp.)
- Steaks halibut (2, 8 oz.)
- White wine (.5 cup)
- Chopped garlic (1 tsp.)
- Butter (.25 cup)
- Salt & pepper (to your liking)
- Capers with liquid (3 tbsp.)

Preparation Instructions:
1. Use the medium-high heat setting, and warm up some olive oil in a large skillet. Sear the steaks on all sides. Transfer to a dish, and place it to the side for now.
2. Add the wine into the pan to break the browned bits from the bottom. Simmer until it is reduced in volume. Stir in the butter, salt, black pepper, garlic, and capers.
3. Simmer the sauce for a minute, and add the steaks into the mixture.
4. Cook until the fish easily flakes using a fork. Serve immediately.

Lemon Garlic Shrimp & Veggies

Serving Yields: 4
Nutritional Count (each portion):
- Calories: 217
- Carbs: 16.7
- Protein: 25.5
- Total Fat: 6.3

Ingredients Needed:
- Olive oil (4 tsp., divided)
- Red bell peppers (2 large)
- Fresh asparagus (2 lb.)
- Lemon zest (2 tsp.)
- Salt (.5 tsp., divided)
- Garlic (5 minced cloves)
- Raw shrimp (26–30 per pound, 1 lb.)
- Reduced-sodium chicken broth (1 cup)
- Cornstarch (1 tsp.)
- Lemon juice (2 tbsp.)
- Freshly chopped parsley (to your liking)

Preparation Instructions:
1. Trim and cut the asparagus into 1-inch lengths. Dice the peppers. Peel and devein the shrimp.
2. Warm up 2 teaspoons oil in a pan using medium-high temperature setting.
3. Toss in the lemon zest, bell peppers, asparagus, and .25 teaspoon of salt. Simmer and stir occasionally for about 6 minutes. Take the veggies out of the pan. Cover with a layer of foil to keep it warm for now.
4. Pour in the rest of the oil and garlic to the skillet; sauté for about 30 seconds.
5. Toss in the shrimp and simmer for 1 minute.
6. Whisk the cornstarch with the broth in a mixing container until it is creamy. Whisk well and pour into the pan with the remainder of the salt.
7. Simmer until the sauce has slightly thickened.
8. Toss in the shrimp. Simmer for 2 minutes until the shrimp is pink.
9. Remove the pan from the burner. Stir in the parsley and lemon juice.
10. Serve the shrimp and veggies with a portion of the delicious sauce.

Pan-Seared Salmon

Serving Yields: 4

Nutritional Count (each portion):
- Calories: 371
- Carbs: 1.7
- Protein: 33.7
- Total Fat: 25.1

Ingredients Needed:
- Salmon fillets (4, 6 oz. each)
- Olive oil (2 tbsp.)
- Salt & pepper (.125 tsp. each)
- Capers (2 tbsp.)
- Lemon (4 slices)

Preparation Instructions:
1. Warm up a heavy skillet for about 3 minutes using the medium-heat setting.
2. Lightly spritz the salmon with olive oil. Arrange it in the pan, and increase the temperature setting to high.
3. Sear for approximately 3 minutes. Sprinkle with the salt, pepper, and capers.
4. Flip the salmon over. Cook for another 5 minutes or until browned the way you like it.
5. Garnish with lemon slices and serve.

Penne with Shrimp

Serving Yields: 8
Nutritional Count (each portion):
- Calories: 385
- Carbs: 48.5
- Protein: 24.5
- Total Fat: 8.5

Ingredients Needed:
- Penne pasta (16 oz. pkg.)
- Salt (.25 tsp.)
- Olive oil (2 tbsp.)
- Red onion (.25 cup)
- Garlic (1 tbsp.)
- White wine (.25 cup)
- Diced tomatoes (2/14.5 oz. cans)
- Shrimp (1 lb.)
- Grated parmesan cheese (1 cup)

Preparation Instructions:
1. Peel and devein the shrimp. Dice the red onion and garlic.
2. Sprinkle the salt into a large pot of water. Place on the stovetop and set to boil. Toss the pasta into the rolling water and cook (9 to 10 min.) before draining.
3. Empty the oil into a skillet. Warm up using the medium-heat setting.
4. Stir in the onions and garlic. Sauté until tender. Pour in the tomatoes and wine. Cook for another 10 minutes. Stir occasionally.
5. Fold in the shrimp and continue cooking for 5 minutes or until it's opaque.
6. Combine the pasta and shrimp together, and top it off with the cheese to serve.

Salmon With Warm Tomato-Olive Salad

Serving Yields: 4
Nutritional Count (each portion):
- Calories: 433
- Carbs: 10
- Protein: 38
- Total Fat: 26

Ingredients Needed:
- Salmon fillets (4, approx. 4 oz., 1.25-inches thick)
- Celery (1 cup)
- Medium tomatoes (2)
- Fresh mint (.25 cup)
- Kalamata olives (.5 cup)
- Garlic (.5 tsp.)
- Salt (1 tsp.)
- Apple cider vinegar (1 tbsp. (+) 1 tsp.)
- Red pepper flakes (.25 tsp.)
- Honey (1 tbsp.)
- Olive oil (5 tbsp. + more for brushing)

Preparation Instructions:
1. Slice the tomatoes and celery into 1-inch pieces, and mince the garlic. Chop the mint and the olives.
2. Warm up the oven using the broiler setting.
3. Whisk 2 tbsp olive oil, 1 tsp vinegar, honey, red pepper flakes, and 1 tsp salt. Brush onto the salmon.

4. Line the broiler pan with aluminum foil. Spritz the pan lightly with oil, and add the fillets with the skin side down.
5. Broil for 4 to 6 minutes until well done.
6. Meanwhile, make the tomato salad. Mix .5 teaspoon of salt with the garlic.
7. Prepare a small saucepan on the stovetop using the medium-high heat setting.
8. Pour in the rest of the oil. Add the garlic mixture, olives, and 1 tablespoon vinegar. Simmer for 3 minutes.
9. Prepare the serving dishes. Pour the bubbly mixture.

Scallops Provencal

Serving Yields: 8

Nutritional Count (each portion):
- Calories: 117
- Carbs: 5.8
- Protein: 13.9
- Total Fat: 3.7

Ingredients Needed:
- Butter (2 tbsp.)
- Sea scallops (1 lb.)
- Small onion (1)
- Mushrooms (.5 lb.)
- Clove of garlic (1 minced)
- Tomatoes (2 medium)
- Salt (.5 tsp.)
- Chopped dried tarragon (.5 tsp.)
- Dried rosemary (.25 tsp.)
- White pepper (1 pinch)

- Frozen-cooked small-sized shrimp (.25 lb.)
- White wine vinegar (2 tsp.)
- Optional: Dry white wine (.25 cup)
- Ketchup (2 tbsp.)

Preparation Instructions:

1. Add the scallops to a colander. Rinse and drain. Finely chop the onions, mushrooms, and peeled tomatoes.
2. Add the butter in a skillet to melt using the medium-high heat setting. Lightly brown the scallops in batches. Remove to individual casseroles or lightly buttered baking shells.
3. Fold in the mushrooms and onions into the skillet. Sauté until the onion is softened and begins to brown.
4. Toss in the garlic, tomatoes, ketchup, wine, salt, tarragon, rosemary, and white pepper.
5. Once boiling, reduce the temperature setting to low to simmer for about 15 minutes. Uncover it and continue cooking until thick (3 min.). Mix in shrimp and vinegar.
6. Dump the sauce over the scallops.
7. Bake in until the sauce bubbles and begins to brown at the edges (10 min.). Sprinkle parsley and serve.

Spanish Moroccan Fish

Serving Yields: 12
Nutritional Count (each portion):
- Calories: 268
- Carbs: 12.6
- Protein: 41.7
- Total Fat: 5.1

Ingredients Needed:
- Vegetable oil (1 tbsp.)
- Onion (1)
- Garlic (1 clove)
- Garbanzo beans (15 oz. can)
- Red bell peppers (2)
- Large carrot (1)
- Tomatoes (3)
- Olives (4)
- Fresh parsley (.25 cup)
- Ground cumin (.25 cup)
- Paprika (3 tbsp.)
- Chicken bouillon granules (2 tbsp.)
- Cayenne pepper (1 tsp.)
- Salt (to taste)
- Tilapia fillets (5 lb.)

Preparation Instructions:
1. Finely chop the onion, tomatoes, garlic, olives, and parsley. Rinse and drain the garbanzo beans. Slice the carrots and bell peppers.
2. Warm up the oil in a pan using the medium-heat setting.
3. Add in the garlic and onions. Saute until softened (5 min.).
4. Toss in the bell peppers, olives, tomatoes, carrots, and beans.
5. Simmer for about 5 more minutes.
6. Sprinkle with paprika, cumin, parsley, chicken bouillon, and the cayenne over the veggies.
7. Dust it with salt, and stir the vegetables. Place the fish into the pan and pour in just enough water to cover the fish.
8. Set the temperature to low. Cook until the fish is flaky or about 40 minutes.

Tilapia Feta Florentine

Serving Yields: 4

Nutritional Count (each portion):
- Calories: 258
- Carbs: 7.3
- Protein: 28
- Total Fat: 13.4

Ingredients Needed:
- Olive oil (2 tsp.)
- Chopped onion (.25 cup)
- Clove of garlic (1 minced
- Fresh spinach (2, 9 oz. bags)
- Sliced Kalamata olives (.25 cup)
- Crumbled feta cheese (2 tbsp.)
- Grated lemon rind (.5 tsp.)
- Salt (.5 tsp.)
- Dried oregano (.25 cup)
- White pepper (.125 cup)
- Tilapia fillets (1 lb.)
- Butter (2 tbsp. melted)
- Lemon juice (2 tsp.)
- Paprika (1 pinch or to taste)
- *Also needed*: 9x13-inch baking dish

Preparation Instructions:

1. Heat up the oven to 400° Fahrenheit.
2. Warm up the oil in a pan using the medium temperature setting. Sauté and stir the garlic and onions in the hot oil about 5 minutes until the onion is softened.
3. Fold the spinach into the skillet. Cook and stir until spinach is wilted and cooked through for 5 more minutes. Stir olives, feta cheese, lemon rind, salt, and oregano, and add white pepper to the spinach. Cook until the feta cheese has melted and flavors have blended for about 5 more minutes.
4. Spread spinach mixture into the baking dish. Arrange tilapia fillets over the spinach mixture. Combine the butter and lemon juice in a small mixing dish. Drizzle over the fish and sprinkle with paprika.
5. Bake until it is opaque and flakes easily, 20 to 25 minutes.

Pork Options

Greek Honey & Lemon Pork Chops

Serving Yields: 4
Nutritional Count (each portion):
- Calories: 257
- Carbs: 10
- Protein: 29
- Total Fat: 10

Ingredients Needed:
- Pork rib chops (4)
- Salt (.5 tsp.)
- Cayenne pepper (.25 tsp.)

- Lemon juice (2 tbsp.)
- Freshly cut mint (1 tbsp.)
- Honey (2 tbsp.)
- Shredded lemon peel (2 tbsp.)
- Olive oil (1 tbsp.)

Preparation Instructions:
1. Remove all fat from the pork chops. Snip the fresh mint, and shred the lemon peel.
2. Slice the chops into 1-inch thick chunks, and put them into a large resealable plastic bag.
3. Whisk the rest of the fixings and pour over the pork. Seal the bag.
4. Rotate the bag a few times and let it marinate for about 4 hours.
5. When it's ready to cook, prepare the grill. Grease the grilling rack with oil. Preheat using the medium-hcat setting.
6. Arrange the chops on the grilling rack. Grill for 5 to 6 minutes on each side. The meat thermometer should reach 160° Fahrenheit.
7. Serve immediately.

Grilled Pork Loin

Serving Yields: 4
Nutritional Count (each portion):
- Calories: 152
- Carbs: 2
- Protein: 6
- Total Fat: 14

Ingredients Needed:
- Boneless pork loin (1, cut into 3 large slices)
- Olive oil (.33 cup)
- Lemon juice (fresh (.25 cup)
- Parsley (2 tbsp.)
- Oregano (1 tbsp.)
- Garlic (1 minced clove)
- Sea salt (.5 tsp.)
- Black pepper, coarse, ground (.5 tsp.)
- *Also needed:* Shallow glass baking dish

Preparation Instructions:
1. Slice the pork into three large slices and arrange in the baking dish.
2. Prepare the marinade and add to the prepared pork.
3. Cover the container with a layer of plastic wrap. Chill and marinate in the fridge for approximately 4 to 6 hours.
4. Warm up the grill using medium heat.
5. Discard the marinade and arrange the pork on the grill.
6. Cook for 8 to 10 minutes per side (The internal temperature to get it well done is 155° to 160° Fahrenheit).
7. Once it's done, remove from grill. Cool it for 5 to 10 minutes before serving.

Mediterranean Pork Chops

Serving Yields: 4

Nutritional Count (each portion):
- Calories: 161
- Carbs: 1
- Protein: 25
- Total Fat: 5

Ingredients Needed:
- Boneless or bone-in pork loin chops (4, .5-inch cut)
- Salt (.25 tsp.)
- Rosemary, dried (1 tsp.) or fresh (1 tbsp.)
- Black pepper (.25 tsp.)
- Minced garlic (1.5 tsp.)

Preparation Instructions:
1. Warm up the oven to 425° Fahrenheit.
2. Prepare the chops to your liking using the salt and pepper. Set to the side.
3. Whisk the rosemary and garlic together. Rub into the pork chops.
4. Prepare a roasting pan with a layer of aluminum foil. Arrange the chops in the pan, and put them into the oven.
5. Lower the temperature setting to 350° Fahrenheit. Roast for 25 minutes.
6. Serve right away.

Other Options

Chicken-Fried Steak

Serving Yields: 4
Nutritional Count (each portion):
- Calories: 791
- Carbs: 71.1
- Protein: 47
- Total Fat: 34.3

Ingredients Needed:
- Beef cube steaks (4, .5 lb. each)
- All-purpose flour (2 cups + .25 cup)
- Bak. powder (2 tsp.)
- Bak. soda (1 tsp.)
- Salt (.75 tsp.)
- Black pepper (1 tsp
- Buttermilk (1.5 cups)
- Egg (1)
- Hot pepper sauce (1 tbsp.)
- Garlic cloves (2)
- Vegetable shortening (3 cups)
- Milk (4 cups)
- Black pepper & Kosher salt (as desired)
- *Also needed:* Deep cast iron skillet

Preparation Instructions:

1. Mince the cloves of garlic. Prepare the steaks with a meat mallet to reach about .25-inch thickness.
2. Add about 2 cups of flour into a shallow bowl.
3. In a separate dish, whisk the black pepper, salt, baking soda, and powder.
4. Pour in the hot sauce, buttermilk, egg, and garlic.
5. Dip and coat each of the steaks in the flour, in the batter, and in the flour again. Be sure each steak is coated well with the dry flour.
6. Warm up the shortening in the skillet (325°Fahrenheit).
7. Fry the steaks to your liking (3 to 5 min. on each side).
8. Place the steaks on a platter with a layer of paper towels to drain the unwanted grease. Reserve .25 cup of the liquid and most of the solid pieces of meat.
9. Switch the skillet to the medium-low heat setting with the last of the oil.
10. Whisk the rest of the flour into the hot pan. Use a spatula to combine the tasty browned solids into the gravy.
11. Pour in the milk. Change the heat setting to medium. Simmer to thicken (6 to 7 min.). Dust with some salt and pepper.
12. Serve the steaks with a portion of gravy.

Mediterranean Farfalle

Serving Yields: 7
Nutritional Count (each portion):
- Calories: 700
- Carbs: 39.4
- Protein: 26.9
- Total Fat: 48

Ingredients Needed:

- Farfalle pasta (12 oz. pkg.)
- Chorizo sausage (1 lb. crumbled)
- Fresh basil leaves (.25 cup)
- Pine nuts (.5 cup)
- Garlic (2 cloves)
- Red wine (3/8 cup)
- Diced tomato (1 cup)
- Grated parmesan cheese (.5 cup)
- Olive oil (.5 cup)

Preparation Instructions:

1. Dice the basil into thin pieces. Mince the garlic. Cook the pasta in the boiling and salted water until al dente.
2. Meanwhile, brown the ham using the medium-heat setting on the stovetop. Toss in the nuts to brown. Watch closely to prevent scorching. Fold in the garlic, and remove from the hot burner.
3. Add the pasta to a colander and drain the pasta. Toss with the cheese, tomatoes, ham mixture, and basil.
4. Whisk the vinegar and oil to pour over the pasta. Toss well and serve.

Mixed Spice Burgers

Serving Yields: 6

Nutritional Count (each portion):
- Calories: 192
- Carbs: 3
- Protein: 32
- Total Fat: 9

Ingredients Needed:
- Medium onion (1)
- Parsley (3 tbsp.)
- Clove of garlic (1)
- Ground allspice (.75 tsp.)
- Pepper (.75 tsp.)
- Ground nutmeg (.25 tsp.)
- Cinnamon (.5 tsp.)
- Salt (.5 tsp.)
- Fresh mint (2 tbsp.)
- 90% lean ground beef (1.5 lb.)
- *Optional*: Cold Tzatziki sauce

Preparation Instructions:
1. Finely chop the onion and parsley. Whisk the nutmeg, salt, cinnamon, pepper, allspice, minced garlic cloves, minced mint, parsley, and the onion.
2. Add the beef and prepare six 2x4-inch oblong patties.
3. Use the medium-heat setting to grill the patties or broil 4 inches from the heat source for 4 to 6 minutes per side.
4. When it's done, the meat thermometer will register 160° Fahrenheit. Serve with the sauce if desired.

Philly Cheesesteak Sandwich With Garlic Mayo

Serving Yields: 4

Nutritional Count (each portion):
- Calories: 935
- Carbs: 49.6
- Protein: 35.3
- Total Fat: 66.4

Ingredients Needed:
- Olive oil (1 tbsp.)
- Mayonnaise (1 cup)
- Garlic (2 cloves)
- Beef round steak (1 lb.)
- Green bell peppers (2)
- Onions (2)
- Salt & pepper (as desired)
- Hoagie rolls (4)
- Shredded mozzarella cheese (8 oz. pkg.)
- Dried oregano (1 tsp.)

Preparation Instructions:
1. Whisk the minced garlic and mayonnaise. Cover and refrigerate.
2. Cut the onions into rings. Slice the steak into thin strips and the peppers into .25-inch strips. Slice the hoagies lengthwise and toast.
3. Warm up the oven to reach 500° Fahrenheit.

4. Pour oil into the skillet on the medium-heat temperature setting. Sauté the beef until golden brown and sprinkle with salt and pepper. Stir in the onions green peppers.
5. Sauté until the veggies are tender, and remove them from the heat.
6. Prepare the buns with garlic mayonnaise.
7. Portion the beef onto the buns with a sprinkle of oregano and the cheese. Place each of the sandwiches on a baking tray.
8. Warm up the oven and toast until the cheese is slightly browned the way you like it.

Roasted Veggie Pasta

Serving Yields: 3

Nutritional Count (each portion):
- Calories: 456
- Carbs: 66.7
- Protein: 16.8
- Total Fat: 14.6

Ingredients Needed:
- Fresh asparagus (.25 lb.)
- Red bell pepper (2 sliced)
- Crimini mushrooms (.25 lb. sliced)
- Roasted garlic cloves (10 chopped)
- Tomato (.5 of 1, quartered)
- Chopped fresh rosemary (.5 tsp.)
- Chopped fresh oregano (.5 tsp.)
- Olive oil (2 tbsp.)

- Dry fettuccini noodles (8 oz.)
- Grated Parmesan cheese (.25 cup)
- Tapenade (2 tbsp.)

Preparation Instructions:

1. Warm the oven to 350° Fahrenheit.
2. Trim the asparagus and slice diagonally into 4-inch segments.
3. Combine the mushrooms, asparagus, bell pepper, tomatoes, and roasted garlic. Sprinkle with rosemary and oregano and a drizzle of oil.
4. Set a timer and bake for 15 minutes.
5. Prepare a large cooking pot of lightly salted water. Once it is boiling, add the pasta and simmer until al dente (8 to 10 min.).
6. Drain the pasta. Toss to your liking with the parmesan cheese, roasted vegetables, and tapenade.

Sweet Sausage Marsala

Serving Yields: 6
Nutritional Count (each portion):
- Calories: 509
- Carbs: 66.1
- Protein: 21.9
- Total Fat: 16.1

Ingredients Needed:
- Italian sausage links (1 lb.)
- Red & green bell pepper (1 medium of each)
- Tomatoes (14.5 oz. can)
- Onion (.5 of 1 large)
- Garlic (.5 tsp.)

- Oregano (.125 tsp.)
- Black pepper (.125 tsp.)
- Marsala wine (1 tbsp.)
- Water (.33 cup)
- Uncooked bow-tie pasta (16 oz.)

Preparation Instructions:

1. Slice the onion and green peppers. Dice the tomatoes or purchase them precut. Mince the garlic.
2. Prepare a large pan of boiling water, about half-full. Toss in the pasta and simmer (8 to 10 min.).
3. Meanwhile, add the sausage to a medium skillet and pour in some water. Set using the medium-high heat temperature. Put a top on the pot and simmer for 8 minutes.
4. When the pasta is done, drain into a colander and set aside.
5. Drain the water from the sausage, and return it to the skillet. Stir in the wine, onions, garlic, and peppers. Simmer for about 5 minutes using the medium-high temperature setting or until done.
6. Place the tomatoes and sprinkle with oregano and some black pepper.
7. Stir and fold in the pasta. Transfer the pan from the heat and serve.

Chapter 5: Snack Favorites

Chocolate Almond Butter Fruit Dip

Serving Yields: 14
Nutritional Count (each portion):
- Calories: 115
- Carbs: 8
- Protein: 4
- Total Fat: 6

Ingredients Needed:
- Plain Greek yogurt (1 cup)
- Almond butter (.5 cup)
- Chocolate-hazelnut spread (.33 cup)
- Vanilla (1 tsp.)
- Honey (1 tbsp.)
- Freshly sliced fruits
- *Also needed:* Blender or food processor

Preparation Instructions:
1. Whisk each of the fixings in a mixing container, except for the fruit of your choice.
2. You can also use a blender; just cover and pulse until smooth.
3. Serve with fruits such as bananas, apples, apricots, or pears.

Date Wraps

Serving Yields: 16
Nutritional Count (each portion):
- Calories: 35
- Carbs: 6
- Protein: 2
- Total Fat: 1

Ingredients Needed:
- Whole pitted dates (16)
- Thinly sliced prosciutto (16 pieces)
- Black pepper (as desired)

Preparation Instructions:
1. Wrap one of the prosciutto slices around each of the dates.
2. When done, serve with a shake of freshly cracked black pepper.

5-Berry Compote With Orange & Mint Infusion

Serving Yields: 8
Nutritional Count (each portion):
- Calories: 203
- Carbs: 34
- Protein: 1
- Total Fat: 0

Ingredients Needed:
- Water (.5 cup)
- Orange pekoe tea bags (3)
- Fresh mint (3, 4-inch sprigs)
- Golden raspberries (1 cup)
- Strawberries (1 cup)
- Pomegranate juice (.5 cup)
- Blueberries (1 cup)
- Sweet cherries (1 cup)
- Red raspberries (1 cup)
- Blackberries (1 cup)
- Sauvignon Blanc (1-milliliter bottle)
- Sugar (.66 cup)
- Vanilla (1 tsp.)
- *Optional:* Fresh mint sprigs

Preparation Instructions:
1. Remove the pits and slice the cherries into halves. Discard the hull from the strawberries and slice lengthwise into halves.
2. For infusion, use a small saucepan of boiling water. Add three sprigs of mint and the tea bags. Stir until the mint wilts. Put a lid on the pan and remove from the heated burner. Wait for about 10 minutes.
3. Use a large mixing container to combine the strawberries, golden raspberries, blackberries, blueberries, red raspberries, and cherries.
4. Use a medium saucepan to prepare the syrup. Add the wine, pomegranate juice, and sugar. Pour the infusion through a fine-mesh sieve into the pan with the wine.
5. Squeeze the tea bags and toss in with the mint sprigs. Simmer until the sugar is dissolved, and take the pan off the heat. Stir in the vanilla. Let it cool to room temperature (5 to 10 min.).

6. Pour the tea mixture over the fruit. Cover with a layer of plastic wrap and store in the fridge for at least 2 hours.
7. Spoon the compote into shallow bowls and serve. Garnish with mint sprigs.
8. *Note*: Be sure to use fresh berries for the best results. You can also substitute 3.5 cups white grape juice for the Sauvignon Blanc wine, and reduce the portion of sugar to .33 cup.
9. *Nutrition per serving with the substitution*: Same as above except for 166 calories and 40 g carbohydrates.

Greek Baklava Bars

Serving Yields: 32 bars
Nutritional Count (each portion):
- Calories: 180
- Carbs: 20
- Protein: 2
- Total Fat: 10

Ingredients Needed:
- Unsalted butter, softened (.5 cup + .33 cup + 3 tbsp.)
- Packed brown sugar (.5 cup + 1.5 tbsp.)
- Vanilla (1 tsp.)
- Lemon peel (1 tsp.)
- Egg (1)
- All-purpose flour (1.5 cups)
- Pistachio nuts (.75 cup)
- Walnuts (1 cup)
- Granulated sugar (.5 cup)
- Cinnamon (1.5 tsp. + .5 tsp.)
- Salt (25 tsp.)
- Baked miniature phyllo dough shells (1, 1.9 oz. pkg.)

- Honey (.5 cup)
- Lemon juice (1 tsp.)
- Allspice (.125 tsp.)
- Ground cloves (.125 tsp.)
- Vanilla (1.5 tsp.)
- Honey
- Pistachio nuts
- *Also needed:* 13x9x2-inch baking pan

Preparation Instructions:

1. Warm up the oven to reach 350° Fahrenheit.
2. Spritz the pan with cooking oil spray. Grate the lemon peel. Chop the nuts.
3. Beat .5 cup butter, .5 cup brown sugar, 1 teaspoon vanilla, and the lemon peel using an electric mixer (medium-high) until creamy smooth. Whisk in the egg. Slowly, mix in the flour until combined.
4. With greased hands, press the dough into the greased baking pan. Set the timer and bake for 10 minutes.
5. Meanwhile, for the nut topping, stir together walnuts, .75 cup of the pistachio nuts, granulated sugar, cinnamon, and salt. Using a fork, mix in the 1/3 cup butter until the mixture is crumbly. Sprinkle over the warm crust. Crumble the phyllo shells. Bake it for 18 to 20 minutes more or until golden.
6. Make the glaze in a microwave-safe bowl by combining 1/2 cup honey, 3 tbsp butter, 1.5 tbsp brown sugar, lemon juice, .5 teaspoon ground cinnamon, allspice, and cloves.
7. Cook uncovered, on 100% power (high) for 1 minute or until the butter melts. Stir in the 1.5 teaspoons vanilla.
8. Drizzle the glaze evenly over the hot mixture in the baking pan. Cool while still in the pan using a wire rack.
9. Use a sharp knife and slice into 16 bars. Cut each bar diagonally in half.

Place on a serving platter and drizzle with additional honey. Sprinkle with additional pistachio nuts.
10. Put the bars into a closed container (single layers) in the fridge up to 3 days. You can also freeze the bars for up to 3 months.

Pistachio No-Bake Snack Bars

Serving Yields: 8 bars

Nutritional Count (each portion):
- Calories: 220
- Carbs: 26
- Protein: 6
- Total Fat: 12

Ingredients Needed:
- Pitted dates (20)
- No-shell roasted & salted pistachios (1.25 cups)
- Rolled old-fashioned oats (1 cup)
- Pistachio butter (2 tbsp.)
- Unsweetened applesauce (.25 cup)
- Vanilla extract (1 tsp.)
- *Also needed*: 8x8 baking dish & food processor with a metal blade

Preparation Instructions:
1. Toss the dates into a mixing dish and pulse until pureed (30 to 45 sec.).
2. Toss in the oats and pistachios. Pulse in 15-second intervals (two to three times) to reach a crumbly, coarse consistency.
3. Pour in the applesauce, pistachio butter, and vanilla extract into the processor. Pulse until the dough is slightly sticky (20 to 30 sec.).

4. Prepare the pan with a layer of baking paper.
5. Use a spatula to transfer the dough into the pan. Press down firmly to evenly distribute the dough into the pan using a second layer of parchment paper.
6. Lift the paper and place the rest of the pistachios onto the top of the dough.
7. Place the pan in the freezer with parchment paper on top and freeze for at least 1 hour before cutting.
8. Slice into eight bars and store in the refrigerator for up to a week.
9. *Note*: To make pistachio butter, take 1 cup of shelled pistachios and add to a food processor with 1 teaspoon vanilla extract. Pulse for 3 to 4 minutes, scraping down the sides as needed, until smooth.

Yogurt & Olive Oil Brownies

Serving Yields: 12
Nutritional Calorie Count: 150

Ingredients Needed:
- Olive oil (.25 cup)
- Eggs (2)
- Low-fat Greek yogurt (.25 cup)
- Sugar (.75 cup)
- Vanilla extract (1 tsp.)
- Flour (.5 cup)
- Cocoa powder (.33 cup + 1-2 tbsp., more as desired)
- Baking powder (.25 tsp.)
- Salt (.25 tsp.)
- Chopped walnuts (.33 cup)
- *Also needed:* 9-inch square pan

Preparation Instructions:
1. Warm up the oven to reach 350° Fahrenheit.
2. Combine the sugar, vanilla, and oil using a wooden spoon. Whisk the eggs and add to the yogurt mixture.
3. In a separate mixing container, sift or whisk the flour, salt, cocoa powder, and baking powder. Stir in the olive oil mixture and the nuts and mix again.
4. Cover the pan with wax paper. Pour the brownie mixture into the pan.
5. Bake for about 25 minutes. Let it cool thoroughly before removing the wax paper. Slice into squares.
6. Top it off with a portion of fresh berries of your choice. (Add the extra calories to your calculation.)

Dips & Spreads

Garlic Garbanzo Bean Spread
Serving Yields: 1.5 cups, 2 tbsp. each:
Nutritional Count (each portion):
- Calories: 114
- Carbs: 6
- Protein: 1
- Total Fat: 10

Ingredients Needed:
- Chickpeas or garbanzo beans (15 oz. can)
- Olive oil (.5 cup)
- Green onion (1, cut into 3 pieces)

- Lemon juice (1 tbsp.)
- Garlic cloves (1–2, peeled)
- Salt (.25 tsp.)
- Freshly minced parsley (2 tbsp.)
- Baked pita chips and assorted fresh veggies
- *Also needed:* Food Processor

Preparation Instructions:
1. Combine the chickpeas or garbanzo beans, oil, parsley, lemon juice, garlic, salt, and green onion.
2. Add the ingredients into the blender and process until mixed.
3. Empty it into a dish and store in the fridge until it's time to eat.
4. Enjoy with pita chips and veggies. You can also use a crispy bread choice with a portion of the delicious mixture.

Spiced Sweet Roasted Red Pepper Hummus

Serving Yields: 8
Nutritional Count (each portion):
- Calories: 64
- Carbs: 9.6
- Protein: 2.5
- Total Fat: 2.2

Ingredients Needed:
- Garbanzo beans (15 oz. can)
- Lemon juice (3 tbsp.)
- Roasted red peppers (4 oz. jar)
- Tahini (1.5 tbsp.)
- Garlic (1 clove)
- Cayenne pepper (.5 tsp.)

- Salt (.25 tsp.)
- Ground cumin (.5 tsp.)
- Fresh parsley (1 tbsp.)

Preparation Instructions:
1. Drain and rinse the beans. Mince the garlic and chop the parsley.
2. Prepare all of the fixings in a food processor or blender.
3. When fluffy and smooth; add to a serving dish for at least 1 hour.
4. Return to the room temperature when it is time to serve.

Chapter 6: Delicious Desserts

Baked Quince With Cinnamon

Serving Yields: 6
Nutritional Count (each portion):
- Calories: 144
- Carbs: 22
- Protein: 0.7
- Total Fat: 5.1

Ingredients Needed:
- Quince, unpeeled (3)
- Whole cloves (18)
- Water (1.5 cups)
- Port wine (.5 cup)
- Cinnamon sticks (3)
- White sugar (.33 cup)
- *Optional:* Heavy cream, whipped (.33 cup)

Preparation Instructions:

1. Warm the oven to reach 375° Fahrenheit.
2. Wash and cut out the core of the quince. Slice it into halves. Press 3 of the cloves into each half and add to a roasting pan with the cut-side facing downward.
3. Pour in the wine, water, and cinnamon sticks. Sprinkle the sugar over the tasty fruit.
4. Bake until lightly browned (35 to 40 min.). Turn the half-baked fruit right-side up. Bake for another 10 minutes.
5. Take the pan from the oven and slightly cool. Place on a serving dish with the cooking juices and a dollop of whipped cream.
6. *Cooking tip:* It is always much easier if you use a layer of aluminum foil under the fruit before baking. It will make the cleanup task much simpler.

Chia Greek Yogurt Pudding

Serving Yields: 4
Nutritional Count (each portion):
- Calories: 263
- Carbs: 21.1
- Protein: 10.4
- Total Fat: 15.9

Ingredients Needed:
- Hemp seeds (2 tbsp.)
- Chia seeds (.66 cup)
- Ground flax seeds (2 tbsp.)

- Cinnamon (1 tsp.)
- Unsweetened soy milk (1 cup)
- Honey (1 tbsp.)
- Greek yogurt (1 cup)
- Vanilla extract (1 tsp.)

Preparation Instructions:
1. Prepare the hemp seeds by removing the outer hulls. Whisk the yogurt and milk in a mixing dish.
2. Pour in the vanilla, cinnamon, honey, flaxseed, and hemp seeds.
3. Lastly, add the chia seeds and stir just enough to mix. Place it in a container and chill for at least 15 minutes.
4. Stir again and chill for another hour. Serve as desired.

Finikia

Serving Yields: 60
Nutritional Count (each portion):
- Calories: 100
- Carbs: 14.9
- Protein: 1.3
- Total Fat: 4.1

Ingredients Needed:
- Butter (.5 cup, softened)
- Corn oil (.5 cup)
- Superfine sugar (.5 cup)
- Zest of orange (1)
- All-purpose flour (2.5 cups)
- Semolina (1.5 cups)

- Cinnamon (1 tsp.)
- Bak. powder (4 tsp.)
- Ground cloves (1 tsp.)
- Lemon juice (2 tsp.)
- Honey (.5 cup)
- Orange juice (.5 cup)
- Water (1 cup)
- Ground flax seeds (2 tbsp.)
- Cinnamon stick (1)
- White sugar (1 cup)
- Walnuts (.5 cup)

Preparation Instructions:

1. Warm up the oven to 350°Fahrenheit. Grease the cookie sheets with a spritz of cooking oil spray.
2. Grate the orange. Cream the superfine sugar with the butter and orange zest. Slowly, stir in the oil. Whisk until fluffy.
3. Mix the cinnamon, flour, cloves, semolina, and baking powder. Whisk with the fluffy mixture alternately with the orange juice.
4. As it thickens, roll it onto a floured cutting board or countertop. Knead into a firm dough and pinch off the dough to make the cookie-sized balls (tablespoon-sized). Arrange the cookies about 2 inches apart on the cookie sheets.
5. Set a timer to bake for 25 minutes. Cool on the baking sheets for about 20 minutes.
6. Prepare the syrup using medium heat, and combine the water, honey, white sugar, cinnamon stick, and lemon juice in a pan. Boil for about 10 minutes.
7. Discard the stick of cinnamon.
8. Dip the cookies into the hot mixture, one at a time, to cover each one completely.

9. Chop the nuts. Put a towel under a wire rack and arrange them to dry with a sprinkle of walnuts.
10. Keep the cookies in a sealed container on the countertop.

Frozen Mint Greek Yogurt

Serving Yields: 16 servings, 1 quart
Nutritional Count (each portion):
- Calories: 84
- Carbs: 15
- Protein: 4
- Total Fat: 1

Ingredients Needed:
- Plain Greek low-fat (2%) yogurt (3 cups)
- Sugar (1 cup)
- Vanilla (2 tsp.)
- Lemon juice (.25 cup)
- Salt (.125 tsp.)
- Snipped fresh mint (2 tbsp.)
- *Also needed:* 1.5 to 2-quart ice cream maker

Preparation Instructions:
1. Whisk the yogurt, salt, vanilla, sugar, and lemon juice until smooth.
2. Freeze the yogurt mixture in the ice cream maker. Toss in the mint and churn.
3. Freeze for 2 to 4 hours in a closed ice cream container.
4. Remove and wait for 5 to 15 minutes before serving.
5. Enjoy as an afternoon snack or evening dessert.

Greek Butter Cookies

Serving Yields: 48
Nutritional Count (each portion):
- Calories: 74
- Carbs: 8.9
- Protein: 0.8
- Total Fat: 4

Ingredients Needed:
- Softened butter (1 cup)
- White sugar (.75 cup)
- Vanilla extract (.5 tsp.)
- Almond extract (.5 tsp.)
- Egg (1)
- All-purpose flour (2.25 cups)
- Confectioners' sugar for rolling (.5 cup)

Preparation Instructions:
1. Warm up the oven to reach 400° Fahrenheit. Grease the cookie pans.
2. Cream the butter with the egg and sugar until creamy smooth. Stir in the almond and vanilla extract.
3. Work in the flour to form the dough, kneading by hand.
4. Grab a teaspoon of dough at a time and roll into cookie balls.
5. Place the cookies about 1 to 2 inches apart on the cookie sheets.
6. Bake until firm and lightly browned (10 min.).
7. Cool completely and dust with confectioners' sugar.

Greek Cheesecake With Yogurt

Serving Yields: 10

Nutritional Count (each portion):
- Calories: 433
- Carbs: 58.2
- Protein: 4.8
- Total Fat: 22.1

Ingredients Needed:
- Digestive/crushed biscuits (9 oz.)
- Melted butter (3.5 oz.)
- Vanilla essence (1 tsp.)
- Cream cheese (16 oz.)
- Greek yogurt (5 oz., thick)
- Icing sugar (4 oz.)
- Honey (2 tbsp.)
- Double cream (9.5 oz.)
- Jam of your choice (.5–1 cup)

Preparation Instructions:
1. Prepare the base by buttering the pan. Toss the biscuits in a food processor. Pulse into crumbs.
2. Pour it into a mixing container, and add the melted butter. Combine thoroughly until the crumbs are totally coated.
3. Pour the mixture into the tin. Press down into the base in an even layer, and chill it in the fridge while you make the filling.
4. Place the Greek yogurt, vanilla, icing sugar, cream cheese, and honey in a mixing container. Prepare using an electric mixer until it's creamy smooth.

5. Pour in the double cream. Beat the mixture until it is incorporated fully.
6. Add the mixture into the biscuit crust, and top the cheesecake with the jam.
7. Store in the fridge overnight for best results or at least 6 hours before serving.

Greek Honey Cake

Serving Yields: 12

Nutritional Count (each portion):
- Calories: 423
- Carbs: 62.3
- Protein: 4.5
- Total Fat: 19.3

Ingredients Needed:
- All-purpose flour (1 cup)
- Bak. powder (1.5 tsp.)
- Cinnamon (.5 tsp.)
- Salt (.25 tsp.)
- Zest of orange (1 tsp.)
- Eggs (3)
- Butter (.75 cup)
- White sugar (.75 cup)
- Milk (.25 cup)
- Walnuts (1 cup)
- Honey (1 cup)
- Water (.75 cup)
- White sugar (1 cup)
- Lemon juice (1 tsp.)
- *Also needed*: 9-inch square pan

Preparation Instructions:

1. Warm up the oven to 350° Fahrenheit.
2. Lightly spritz the baking sheet and dust with flour.
3. Make the syrup. Combine 1 cup of sugar, honey, and water. Simmer for about 5 minutes. Pour in the lemon juice and wait for it to boil. Simmer for 2 minutes.
4. Chop the nuts. Whisk the salt, flour, salt, baking powder, orange rind, and cinnamon.
5. In another mixing container, cream the butter and .75 cup of sugar mixture until fluffy.
6. Whisk the eggs, adding one at a time. Mix in the flour mixture, alternating with the milk until incorporated. Fold in the nuts.
7. Dump the batter into the prepared pan.
8. Bake for 40 to 45 minutes. Cool for approximately 15 minutes while in the pan. Use a sharp knife to slice the cake into rectangular or other shapes.
9. Pour the honey syrup evenly over the cake.

Greek Lemon Cake

Serving Yields: 12
Nutritional Count (each portion):
- Calories: 443
- Carbs: 62.7
- Protein: 7
- Total Fat: 18.8

Ingredients Needed:

- Cake flour (3 cups)
- Salt (.25 tsp.)
- Baking soda (1 tsp.)
- Eggs (6 separated)
- White sugar (2 cups, divided)
- Butter (1 cup, softened)
- Grated lemon zest (2 tsp.)
- Plain whole-milk yogurt (1 cup)
- Lemon juice (2 tbsp.)
- *Also needed:* 10-inch tube pan

Preparation Instructions:

1. Grease the pan.
2. Warm the oven to reach 350° Fahrenheit.
3. Sift or whisk the salt, flour, and baking soda.
4. Whisk the egg whites until soft peaks form. Gradually add in .5 cup of sugar. Whisk until stiff glossy peaks form.
5. Work in the butter and the rest of the sugar in another mixing bowl with an electric mixer until fluffy (3 to 5 min.).
6. Blend in the lemon zest, egg yolks, and juice. Fold in the flour mixture alternately with the yogurt, mixing until well incorporated.
7. Gently fold in the egg whites. Empty the batter into the tube pan.
8. Bake for 50 to 60 min, and cool it in its pan for 10 minutes.
9. Turn it out onto a rack to finish cooling.

Greek Yogurt Bowl With Peanut Butter & Bananas

Serving Yields: 4
Nutritional Count (each portion):
- Calories: 370
- Carbs: 47.7
- Protein: 22.7
- Total Fat: 10.6

Ingredients Needed:
- Medium bananas (2)
- Flaxseed meal (.25 cup)
- Nutmeg (1 tsp.)
- Vanilla flavored Greek yogurt (4 cups)
- Creamy natural peanut butter (.25 cup)

Preparation Instructions:
1. Prepare four serving bowls with the yogurt. Top it with banana slices.
2. Put the peanut butter in a heatproof dish in the microwave to melt for 30 to 40 seconds.
3. Drizzle 1 tbsp of the melted peanut butter over the sliced bananas. Sprinkle with the nutmeg and flaxseed meal. Serve right away and enjoy.

Greek Yogurt Chocolate Mousse

Serving Yields: 4
Nutritional Count (each portion):
- Calories: 328
- Carbs: 25.4
- Protein: 15.2
- Total Fat: 10.4

Ingredients Needed:

- Milk (.75 cup)
- Dark chocolate (3.5 oz.)
- Greek yogurt (2 cups)
- Maple syrup/honey (1 tbsp.)
- Vanilla extract (.5 tsp.)

Preparation Instructions:

1. Empty the milk into a saucepan, and add the finely chopped chocolate.
2. Warm up the milk until the chocolate melts, while not allowing it to boil. Once combined, add the vanilla and honey. Stir well.
3. Add the yogurt into a large bowl and dump the chocolate mixture on top. Mix well and pour into individual glasses or another dish.
4. Chill in the refrigerator for 2 hours.
5. Serve with a portion of the yogurt and several fresh raspberries.
6. The mousse will store well in the refrigerator for 2 days.

Honey-Pistachio Roasted Pears

Serving Yields: 6

Nutritional Count (each portion):

- Calories: 250
- Carbs: 27
- Protein: 3
- Total Fat: 12

Ingredients Needed:
- Ripe medium Bartlett pears (3)
- Pear nectar (.25 cup)
- Honey (3 tbsp.)
- Butter (2 tbsp.)
- Orange zest (1 tsp.)
- Mascarpone cheese (.5 cup)
- Powdered sugar (2 tbsp.)
- Chopped roasted, salted pistachios (.33 cup)

Preparation Instructions:
1. Warm up the oven to 400° Fahrenheit.
2. Peel the pears and remove the cores. Slice into halves. Arrange the pears, cut sides down, in a 2-quart rectangular baking dish.
3. Add the next four ingredients. Roast, uncovered until tender (15 to 25 min.). Spoon the liquid over the pears occasionally.
4. Transfer the pears to serving dishes with a portion of the liquid. Stir together the mascarpone cheese and powdered sugar.
5. Spoon over pears and sprinkle with pistachios. If desired, drizzle with additional honey.

Honey Pistachio Tart

Serving Yields: 8
Nutritional Count (each portion):
- Calories: 523
- Carbs: 57
- Protein: 9
- Total Fat: 6

Ingredients Needed:
- Sugar (.5 cup)
- Honey (.25 cup)
- Water (.25 cup)
- Chopped pistachio nuts (1.5 cups, toasted)
- Bits of mixed dried fruit (.5 cup)
- Orange juice (.25 cup)
- All-purpose flour (2 cups)
- Salt (.25 tsp.)
- Vegetable shortening (.66 cup)
- Water, cold (.25 cup)
- Egg (1)
- Egg yolk (1)
- Coarse sugar
- *Also needed*: 13.5x4-inch oblong tart pan (needs a removable bottom)

Preparation Instructions:

1. Prepare the filling using a saucepan. Mix the water, sugar, and honey. Gently boil until the sugar is dissolved. Lower the temperature setting to medium-low.
2. Simmer with the lid off for about 15 minutes. Stir occasionally.
3. Fold in the pistachios, fruit, and orange juice. Let it boil before lowering the temperature. Simmer until the mixture is slightly thickened (5 min.). Stir and set to the side for now.
4. Prepare the egg pastry in a large mixing container.
5. Whisk the salt and flour. Cut in the shortening until the mixture is pea-sized.
6. In another container, whisk the egg and the .25 cup cold water.
7. Mix the egg mixture and flour mixture using a fork, tossing until the dry fixings are moistened. Break the dough in half, forming each one into a ball.
8. Slightly flatten one ball of pastry into a rectangle.

9. On a lightly floured surface, roll the dough into a (16x6-inch) rectangle. Roll it out. Place in the pan, pressing it up the sides. Add the filling.
10. For the top pastry, just roll out the rest of the pastry ball into a 10-inch square. Slice into .5-inch-wide strips.
11. Weave the strips across the top of filling as desired.
12. Press ends into the rim of pan. Brush egg yolk over the lattice top and sprinkle with sugar.
13. Bake at 375° Fahrenheit for about 35 minutes. (Cover with a piece of aluminum foil if the crust starts to brown too fast.)
14. Cool in the pan on a wire rack. Discard the sides from the baking pan and serve.

Italian Apple Olive Oil Cake

Serving Yields: 12
- Calories: 294
- Carbs: 47.7
- Protein: 5.3
- Total Fat: 11

Ingredients Needed:
- Gala apples (2 large)
- Orange juice, for soaking apples (as needed)
- All-purpose flour (3 cups)
- Cinnamon (.5 tsp.)
- Nutmeg (.5 tsp.)
- Bak. powder (1 tsp.)
- Bak. soda (1 tsp.)

- Sugar (1 cup)
- Olive oil (1 cup)
- Large eggs (2)
- Gold raisins (.66 cup)
- Confectioner's sugar, for dusting
- *Also needed:* 9-inch baking pan

Preparation Instructions:

1. Peel and finely chop the apples. Drizzle the apples with just enough orange juice to prevent browning.
2. Soak the raisins in warm water for 15 minutes and drain well.
3. Sift the baking soda, nutmeg, baking powder, cinnamon, and flour. Place to the side for now.
4. Pour the olive oil and sugar into the bowl of a stand mixer. Mix on the low setting for 2 minutes or until combined well.
5. Blend and break in the eggs one at a time and continue mixing for 2 minutes. The mixture should increase in volume; it should be thick, not runny.
6. Combine all of the ingredients well. Make a well in the center of the flour mixture and add in the olive and sugar mixture.
7. Remove the excess juice from the apples, and drain the raisins that have been soaking. Add them together with the batter, mixing well.
8. Prepare the baking pan with parchment paper. Spoon the batter into the pan and level it with the back of a wooden spoon.
9. Bake it for 45 minutes at 350° Fahrenheit.
10. When ready, remove the cake from the parchment paper and transfer into a serving dish.
11. Dust with confectioner's sugar. Warm up some dark honey to garnish the top.

Low-Fat Apple Cake

Serving Yields: 6
Nutritional Count (each portion):
- Calories: 116
- Carbs: 25.3
- Protein: 2.4
- Total Fat: 1

Ingredients Needed:
- Apples (1.5 lb.)
- Eggs (2)
- Light brown or granulated sugar (.33 cup + 1 tbsp.)
- Grated zest (1 lemon)
- Salt (1 pinch)
- Sifted all-purpose flour (1 cup (–) 1 tbsp.)
- Low-fat milk (.25 cup + 1 tbsp.)
- Baking powder (3 tsp.)
- *Optional:* Sugar to sprinkle on top and icing sugar for dusting
- *Also needed:* 8.5-inch baking pan

Preparation Instructions:

1. Warm the oven ahead of baking time to 350° Fahrenheit.
2. Spritz the pan with a portion of cooking oil spray. Flour the pan and set aside.
3. Place the lemon zest, sugar, eggs, and salt in the bowl of a stand mixer and beat until thick and creamy.
4. Add the baking powder, flour, and milk. Beat until combined well.
5. Peel, core, and thinly slice the apples. Add about 2/3 of the apples into the

batter. Mix well with a wooden spoon.
6. Pour the batter in the greased pan.
7. Arrange the remaining apple slices over the top of the batter, and sprinkle it with 1 tablespoon of brown sugar.
8. Set a timer and bake for 35 minutes. Insert a toothpick into the center of the cake to test for doneness. It is ready when it comes out clean.
9. Sprinkle the cake with powdered sugar and serve.
10. *Note*: It is best to use Granny Smith or Golden Delicious apples.

Popped Quinoa Crunch Bars

Serving Yields: 20
Nutritional Count (each portion):
- Calories: 170
- Carbs: 24
- Protein: 4
- Total Fat: 8

Ingredients Needed:
- Baker's Semi-sweet chocolate bars (4, 4oz. or 16 oz total)
- Dry quinoa (1 cup)
- PB2 (1 tbsp.)
- Vanilla (.5 tsp.)
- *For the peanut butter drizzle:*
- Water (2 tbsp.) + PB2 (2.5 tbsp.)

Preparation Instructions:
1. Chop the chocolate into small bits.
2. Prepare a heavy-bottomed pot using a medium-high temperature setting. Let

it heat up for several minutes.
3. Add the quinoa, .25 cup at a time. Let it sit in the bottom of the pot until you start to hear light popping. Swirl for about a minute until the popping has subsided slightly. Make sure you take it off before it gets brown.
4. Once it has popped, set it to the side for now.
5. Melt the chopped chocolate in a double boiler.
6. Add the quinoa, PB2, melted chocolate, and vanilla to a bowl. Mix well to combine.
7. Prepare a baking sheet with a layer of parchment baking paper. Spread the chocolate quinoa mixture across the top, about .5-inch thick.
8. Stir the peanut butter and drizzle all over the top of your chocolate and quinoa. Swirl it around gently.
9. Place in the fridge until firm or for at least an hour before slicing. Keep in the refrigerator or on the countertop once they are sliced.

Pumpkin Bread

Serving Yields: 24

Nutritional Count (each portion):
- Calories: 263
- Carbs: 40.6
- Protein: 3.1
- Total Fat: 10.3

Ingredients Needed:
- Pumpkin puree (15 oz. can)
- Water (.66 cup)
- Eggs (4)
- Vegetable oil (1 cup)
- White sugar (3 cups)

- All-purpose flour (3.5 cups)
- Baking soda (2 tsp.)
- Nutmeg (1 tsp.)
- Salt (1.5 tsp.)
- Cinnamon (1 tsp.)
- Ground cloves (.5 tsp.)
- Ground ginger (.25 tsp.)
- *Also needed*: 7x3-inch loaf pans (3)

Preparation Instructions:

1. Warm up the oven to 350° Fahrenheit.
2. Grease and lightly flour the three pans.
3. In a large mixing container, combine the eggs, oil, pumpkin puree, water, and sugar until blended well.
4. In another container, whisk the baking soda, salt, flour, cinnamon, cloves, nutmeg, and ginger. Combine all of the fixings and pour into the pans.
5. Set a timer and bake for about 50 minutes.
6. You would know that the loaves are done when a toothpick inserted in the center comes out clean.

Raspberry Fudge Greek Frozen Yogurt

Serving Yields: 16, 1 quart
Nutritional Count (each portion):
- Calories: 115
- Carbs: 22
- Protein: 4
- Total Fat: 1

Ingredients Needed:
- Plain Greek low-fat 2% yogurt (3 cups)
- Sugar (1 cup)
- Freshly squeezed lemon juice (.25 cup)
- Vanilla (2 tsp.)
- Salt (.125 tsp.)
- Raspberry preserves (.25 cup)
- Chocolate-flavor syrup (.25 cup)
- Shaved chocolate and fresh red raspberries
- *Also needed*: 1.5 to 2-quart ice cream maker

Preparation Instructions:
1. Combine the sugar, yogurt, vanilla, lemon juice, and salt. Whisk until it's creamy smooth.
2. Freeze the mixture in the ice cream maker according to the manufacturer's instructions. Swirl in .25 cup of each of the raspberry preserves and chocolate-flavored syrup.
3. Transfer to a closed container. Freeze for 2 to 4 hours. Let it stand at room temperature for 5 to 15 minutes before it's time to serve.
4. Top with shaved chocolate and fresh red raspberries.

Strawberry Greek Frozen Yogurt

Serving Yields: 1 quart
Nutritional Count (each portion):
- Calories: 86
- Carbs: 16
- Protein: 4
- Total Fat: 1

Ingredients Needed:
- 2% plain Greek yogurt (3 cups)
- Fresh lemon juice (.25 cup)
- Sugar (1 cup)
- Vanilla (2 tsp.)
- Salt (.125 tsp.)
- Sliced strawberries (1 cup)
- *Also needed:* 1.5 to 2-quart ice cream maker

Preparation Instructions:
1. Whisk the vanilla, salt, lemon juice, yogurt, and sugar until creamy.
2. Place the mixture in the ice cream maker to prepare.
3. Toss in the sliced berries for the last minute of the cycle.
4. Empty into a container. Freeze for 2 to 4 hours before serving
5. Before serving, let the ice cream sit out at room temperature for about 5 to 15 minutes for best results.

Sweet Ricotta & Strawberry Parfaits

Serving Yields: 6
Nutritional Count (each portion):
- Calories: 157
- Carbs: 18
- Protein: 9
- Total Fat: 6

Ingredients Needed:
- Fresh strawberries (1 lb.)
- Sugar (1 tsp.)
- Freshly cut mint (1 tbsp. + more for the garnish)
- Part-skim ricotta cheese (15 oz. carton)
- Light agave nectar (3 tbsp.)
- Vanilla (.5 tsp.)
- Lemon peel (.25 tsp.)

Preparation Instructions:
1. Trim the berries and slice into halves or quarters. Finely shred the lemon peel.
2. Combine the sugar, strawberries, and 1 tablespoon snipped mint in a mixing container. Stir to combine. Let the berries soften (10 min.).
3. In another mixing container, combine the agave nectar, ricotta, vanilla, and lemon peel. Beat with an electric mixer on medium speed for 2 minutes.
4. Scoop 1 tablespoon of the ricotta mixture into each of six parfait glasses. Top with a large spoonful of the strawberry mixture.
5. Repeat the layers with the remaining ricotta and strawberry mixture. Garnish with additional fresh mint as desired.
6. Serve immediately or cover and chill for up to 4 hours.

Triple-Chocolate Tiramisu

Serving Yields: 12
Nutritional Count (each portion):
- Calories: 256
- Carbs: 17
- Protein: 6
- Total Fat: 18

Ingredients Needed:
- Ladyfingers, split (2, 3 oz. pkg.)
- Brewed espresso or strong coffee (.25 cup)
- Mascarpone cheese (8 oz. carton)
- Whipping cream (1 cup)
- Powdered sugar (.25 cup)
- Vanilla (1 tsp.)
- Chocolate liqueur (.33 cup)
- White chocolate baking squares or white baking bars (1 oz., grated)
- Bittersweet chocolate (1 oz., grated)
- *For the garnish*: Unsweetened cocoa powder
- *Optional*: Chopped chocolate-covered coffee beans
- *Also needed*: 8x8x2-inch baking pan

Preparation Instructions:

1. Line the bottom of the pan with a few of the ladyfingers, breaking apart to fit. Drizzle half of the espresso over ladyfingers. Place it to the side for now.
2. Whisk the whipping cream, mascarpone cheese, powdered sugar, and

vanilla using an electric mixer until stiff peaks form.
3. Fold in the chocolate liqueur until just combined. Spoon about half of the mascarpone mixture over the ladyfingers.
4. Sprinkle white chocolate and bittersweet chocolate over the mascarpone mixture.
5. Top with another layer of ladyfingers.
6. Layer it with the rest of the espresso and mascarpone cheese mixture.
7. Cover and chill in the fridge for at least 6 hours (24 hours is best).
8. Sift a portion of the cocoa powder over the top of the dessert.
9. You can also garnish with cocoa beans.

Watermelon Cubes

Serving Yields: 16
Nutritional Count (each portion):
- Calories: 7
- Carbs: 2
- Protein: 0
- Total Fat: 0

Ingredients Needed:
- Seedless watermelon cubes (16, 1-inch)
- Cucumber (.33 cup)
- Red onion (5 tsp.)
- Fresh mint (2 tsp.)
- Lime juice (.5 to 1 tsp.)
- Cilantro (2 tsp.)

Preparation Instructions:
1. Finely chop the cucumber and onion. Mince the cilantro and mint. Use a measuring spoon or a small melon baller to remove the center of each of the watermelon cubes. Leave a ¼-inch shell. Use the pulp another time.
2. In a small dish, mix the remaining fixings. Spoon into the watermelon cubes and serve.

Smoothies For All Times

Smoothies are an excellent choice for providing your body with essential vitamins, minerals, fiber, protein, and unsaturated fats. You can enjoy them for breakfast or any time you want a delicious beverage.

Try a mixture of these ingredients for a special Mediterranean blend and know some of the benefits of the chosen fixings:

- *Almond Milk*: More almonds are always a great thing, in my opinion. But, you can certainly use your preferred milk for a blueberry smoothie.

- *Almond Butter*: Make a delicious addition by adding nut butter to most of the smoothies. It gives them a bit of bulk.

- *Cinnamon*: Add a touch of sweet spice.

- *Cayenne*: Cayenne makes a tasty smoothie. It doesn't add any flavor, but a sensation of heat along with the sweetness of the other ingredients is something you shouldn't miss. If you do not like the cayenne, try to add some turmeric instead. Turmeric is another great spice to add to your diet!

- *Spinach or leafy greens*: Spinach is an all-time favorite. Kale is another good option for smoothies.
- *Frozen Banana*: Most smoothies need a frozen banana or other frozen base to make them thick, creamy, and cold. Bananas are easily stored in the freezer.

Green Avocado & Apple Smoothie

Serving Yields: 2
Nutritional Count (each portion):
- Calories: 417
- Carbs: 55
- Protein: 9
- Total Fat: 21

Ingredients Needed:
- Spinach (3 cups)
- Granny Smith apple (1 roughly chopped)
- Coconut water (2 cups)
- Avocado (1)
- Banana, frozen for at least 15 minutes (1)
- Chia seeds (3 tbsp.)
- Honey (1 tsp.)

Preparation Instructions:

1. Toss the apple, spinach, and coconut water in a blender. Mix well until creamy smooth.
2. Slice the avocado and add in the banana, chia seeds, and honey. Blend until the mixture is smooth.
3. Pour the smoothie into tall chilled glasses. Serve immediately.

Healthy Breakfast Smoothies Variety Pack

Serving Yields: 1

Nutritional Count (each portion):
- Calories: 137
- Carbs: 29
- Protein: 6
- Total Fat: 0

Ingredients Needed:
- Greek yogurt *or* cashews *or* your choice of skinless nuts (.25 cup)
- Frozen banana (.5 of 1)
- Water (.5 cup)
- Frozen raw fruit (.5 cup)
- Frozen raw vegetable (.5 cup)

Preparation Instructions:

1. Add either the nuts or Greek Yogurt, half of a frozen banana, and the water to a blender.
2. Prepare the fruits and vegetable you will use, and add *one* fruit and *one* vegetable and blend until smooth.
3. Try one of these:
   a. *Green Smoothie*: Avocado & Baby Spinach
   b. *Hot Pink Smoothie:* Beet & Raspberry
   c. *Light Pink Smoothie*: Cauliflower & Strawberry
   d. *Purple Smoothie:* Blueberry & Red Cabbage
   e. *Orange Smoothie:* Orange & Carrot
   f. *Yellow Smoothie:* Mango (or Pineapple) & Butternut Squash

Mediterranean Smoothie Delight

Serving Yields: 2

Nutritional Count (each portion):
- Calories: 168
- Carbs: 39
- Protein: 4
- Total Fat: 1

Ingredients Needed:
- Baby spinach (2 cups)
- Fresh ginger root, minced (1 tsp.)
- Frozen banana (1)
- Small mango (1)

- Beet juice (.5 cup)
- Skim milk or unsweetened almond milk (.5 cup)
- Ice cubes (4–6)

Preparation Instructions:

1. Measure and wash the spinach. Slice the frozen banana.
2. Wash the fresh beets and pat dry.
3. Warm up the oven to reach 375° Fahrenheit.
4. Rub the outside part of beets with a little olive oil. Wrap them in a foil and roast for 50 minutes to 1 hour or until tender.
5. Let the beets cool slightly and peel. Add one beet to the smoothie.
6. Toss all the fixings in a blender and mix until smooth.

The Ultimate Breakfast Smoothie

Serving Yields: 1, 1.5 cups
Nutritional Count (each portion):
- Calories: 300
- Carbs: 40
- Protein: 12.5
- Total Fat: 11

Ingredients Needed:

- Unsweetened almond milk (.5 cup)
- Fresh or frozen banana (1 medium)
- Almond butter (1 tbsp.)

- Chopped mangoes or sliced strawberries or blueberries (.5 cup)
- 2% plain Greek yogurt (.25cup)
- Baby spinach (.5 cup)
- *Optional*:
- Basil leaves (1–2)
- Mint leaves (2–3)
- Ginger, peeled & chopped (.5 tsp.)

Preparation Instructions:

1. Toss all of the fixings into the blender.
2. Mix until creamy smooth and serve.

Chapter 7: Your Special 29-Day Meal Plan & Pyramid Food Options

You will find the recipes for each of these delicious meal suggestions in the previous chapters.

Day 1:

Breakfast: Deep Dish Spinach Quiche: 6 servings (613 calories)

Lunch: Shrimp Orzo Salad: 8 servings (397 calories)

Dinner: Grecian Pasta Chicken Skillet: 4 servings (373 calories)

Snack or Dessert: Chia Greek Yogurt Pudding: 4 servings (263 calories)

Day 2:

Breakfast: Broccoli & Cheese Omelet: 4 servings (229 calories)

Lunch: Chicken Soup: 4 servings (820 calories)

Dinner: Baked Salmon With Dill: 4 servings (251 calories)

Snack or Dessert: Date Wraps: 16 servings (35 calories)

Day 3:

Breakfast: French Toast Delight: 12 servings (123 calories)

Lunch: Chickpea Salad: 4 servings (163 calories)

Dinner: Mediterranean Pork Chops: 4 servings (161 calories)

Snack or Dessert: Greek Yogurt Bowl With Peanut Butter & Bananas: 4 servings (370 calories)

Day 4:

Breakfast: Eggs Baked In Tomatoes: 4 servings (288 calories)

Lunch: Quinoa Black Bean Burger: 5 servings (245 calories)

Dinner: Chicken & Orzo Pasta: 4 servings (462 calories)

Snack or Dessert: Low-Fat Apple Cake: 6 servings (116 calories)

Day 5:

Breakfast: Peanut Butter & Banana Greek Yogurt Bowl: 4 servings (370 calories)

Lunch: Chickpea - Garbanzo Soup: 4 servings (340 calories)

Dinner: Avocado & Tuna Tapas: 4 servings (294 calories)

Snack or Dessert: Greek Baklava Bars: 32 servings (180 calories)

Day 6:

Breakfast: Holiday Breakfast Sausage Casserole: 8 servings (377 calories)

Lunch: Honey Lime Fruit Salad: 8 servings (115 calories)

Dinner: Quick Chicken Marsala: 4 servings (344 calories)

Snack or Dessert: Banana Sour Cream Bread: 32 servings (263 calories)

Day 7:

Breakfast: Crustless Spinach Quiche: 6 servings (309 calories)

Lunch: Lemon Chicken Soup: 4 servings (130 calories)

Dinner: Pan Seared Salmon: 4 servings (371 calories)

Snack or Dessert: Chocolate Almond Butter Fruit Dip: 14 servings (115 calories)

Day 8:

Breakfast: Egg White Scramble With Cherry Tomatoes & Spinach: 4 servings (142 calories)

Lunch: Zucchini - Artichoke & Chicken Salad: 6 servings (312 calories)

Dinner: Greek Honey & Lemon Pork Chops: 4 servings (257 calories)

Snack or Dessert: Raspberry Fudge Greek FrozenYogurt: 16 servings (115 calories)

Day 9:

Breakfast: Basic Crepes: 4 servings (216 calories)

Lunch: Fast Seafood Gumbo: 5 servings (363 calories)

Dinner: Lemon Garlic Shrimp & Veggies: 4 servings (217 calories)

Snack or Dessert: Greek Yogurt Chocolate Mousse: 4 servings (328 calories)

Day 10:

Breakfast: Mediterranean Omelette: 1 serving (303 calories)

Lunch: Hummus & Prosciutto Wraps: 4 servings (345 calories)

Dinner: Salmon With Warm Tomato-Olive Salad: 4 servings (433 calories)

Snack or Dessert: Triple-Chocolate Tiramisu: 12 servings (256 calories)

Day 11:

Breakfast: Feta - Quinoa & Egg Muffins: 12 servings (114 calories)

Lunch: Vegetable Noodle Soup: 4 servings (316 calories)

Dinner: Chicken-Fried Steak: 4 servings (791 calories)

Snack or Dessert: Pistachio No-Bake Snack Bars: 8 servings (220 calories)

Day 12:

Breakfast: Potato Hash With Poached Eggs, Chickpeas & Asparagus: 4 servings (535 calories)

Lunch: Zesty Quinoa Salad: 6 servings (270 calories)

Dinner: Feta Shrimp Skillet: 4 servings (240 calories)

Snack or Dessert: Watermelon Cubes: 16 servings (7 calories)

Day 13:

Breakfast: Baked Eggs & Zoodles with Avocado: 2 servings (633 calories)

Lunch: Linguine With Garlicky Clams & Peas: 4 servings (368 calories)

Dinner: Chicken Breast Cutlets with Capers & Artichokes: 6 servings (408 calories)

Snack or Dessert: Italian Apple Olive Oil Cake: 12 servings (294 calories)

Day 14:

Breakfast: Feta Frittata: 2 servings (203 calories)

Lunch: Arugula Salad: 4 servings (257 calories)

Dinner: Halibut & Capers: 4 servings (284 calories)

Snack or Dessert: Frozen Mint Greek Yogurt: 16 servings (84 calories)

Day 15:

Breakfast: Crustless Spinach Quiche: 6 servings (309 calories)

Lunch: Greek Lentil Soup: 4 servings (357 calories)

Dinner: Lemon Chicken Piccata: 4 servings (421 calories)

Snack or Dessert: Yogurt & Olive Oil Brownies: 12 servings (150 calories)

Day 16:

Breakfast: Delicious Scrambled Eggs: 2 servings (249 calories)

Lunch: Cucumber Salad: 4 servings (68 calories)

Dinner: Super Tender Chicken: 4 servings (420 calories)

Snack or Dessert: Sweet Ricotta & Strawberry Parfaits: 6 servings (157 calories)

Day 17:

Breakfast: Herb - Sausage & Cheese Dutch Baby: 4 servings (287 calories)

Lunch: Fasolakia - Green Green Beans & Potatoes: 4 servings (289 calories)

Dinner: Spanish Moroccan Fish: 12 servings (268 calories)

Snack or Dessert: Honey-Pistachio Roasted Pears: 6 servings (250 calories)

Day 18:

Breakfast: Watermelon Feta & Balsamic Pizza: 4 servings (90 calories)

Lunch: Fruity Curry Chicken Salad: 8 servings (229 calories)

Dinner: Lemon Chicken Skewers: 6 servings (219 calories)

Snack or Dessert: Italian Apple Olive Oil Cake: 12 servings (294 calories)

Day 19:

Breakfast: Quinoa Egg Breakfast Muffin: 12 servings (118 calories)

Lunch: Creamy Italian White Bean Soup: 4 servings (245 calories)

Dinner: Slow Cooked Lemon Chicken: 6 servings (336 calories)

Snack or Dessert: Greek Yogurt Chocolate Mousse: 4 servings (328 calories)

Day 20:

Breakfast: Vegan Gingerbread & Banana Quinoa Breakfast Bake: 8 servings (213 calories)

Lunch: Fried Rice With Spinach - Peppers & Artichokes: 4 servings (244 calories)

Dinner: Slow Cooked Mediterranean Roasted Turkey Breast: 8 servings (333 calories)

Snack or Dessert: Pumpkin Bread: 24 servings (263 calories)

Day 21:

Breakfast: Poached Eggs: 2 servings (72 calories)

Lunch: Nicoise-Style Tuna Salad With Olives & White Beans: 4 servings (548 calories)

Dinner: Feta Chicken Burgers: 6 servings (356 calories)

Snack or Dessert: Greek Lemon Cake: 12 servings (443calories)

Day 22:

Breakfast: Spanish Potato Omelet: 16 servings (101 calories)

Lunch: Chickpea Garbanzo Soup: 4 servings (340 calories)

Dinner: Scallops Provencal: 8 servings (117 calories)

Snack or Dessert: Mediterranean Smoothie Delight: 2 servings (168 calories)

Day 23:

Breakfast: Low-Carb Keto Egg & Ham Muffins: 6 servings (109 calories)

Lunch: Tomato Feta Salad: 4 servings (121 calories)

Dinner: Mixed Spice Burgers: 6 servings (192 calories) & Sweet Slaw: 8 servings (200 calories)

Snack or Dessert: Finikia: 60 servings (100 calories)

Day 24:

Breakfast: Mediterranean Toast: 1 serving (333.7 calories)

Lunch: Red Lentil Soup: 5 servings (290 calories)

Dinner: Sweet Sausage Marsala: 6 servings (509 calories)

Snack or Dessert: Greek Butter Cookies: 48 servings (74 calories)

Day 25:

Breakfast: Shakshuka Classic: 4 servings (179 calories)

Lunch: Skillet Gnocchi with White Beans & Chard: 6 servings (259 calories)

Dinner: Sicilian Olive Chicken: 4 servings (207 calories)

Snack or Dessert: Strawberry Greek Frozen Yogurt: 1 quart (86 calories)

Day 26:

Breakfast: Pumpkin Pancakes: 6 servings (278 calories)

Lunch: Insalata Caprese II Salad: 6 servings (311 calories)

Dinner: Penne with Shrimp: 8 servings (385 calories)

Snack or Dessert: 5-Berry Compote with Orange & Mint Infusion: 8 servings (203 calories)

Day 27:

Breakfast: Greek Omelette Casserole: 12 servings (196 calories)

Lunch: Skillet Gnocchi with White Beans & Chard: 6 servings (259 calories)

Dinner: Philly Cheesesteak Sandwich with Garlic Mayo: 4 servings (935 calories)

Snack or Dessert: Popped Quinoa Crunch Bars: 20 servings (170 calories)

Day 28:

Breakfast: Chia Berry Overnight Oats: 1 serving (526 calories)

Lunch: Chickpea Salad: 4 servings (163 calories)

Dinner: Chicken Sausage Gnocchi: 4 servings (430 calories)

Snack or Dessert: Triple-Chocolate Tiramisu: 12 servings (256 calories)

Day 29:

Breakfast: Breakfast Egg Muffins: 2 servings (308 calories)

Lunch: Quinoa Soup: 4 servings (560 calories)

Dinner: Italian Chicken Skillet: 4 servings (515 calories)

Snack or Dessert: Green Avocado & Apple Smoothie: 2 servings (417 calories)

Now, just enjoy!

The Pyramid Options
Overall: Yes, plenty of water is at the head of the list for every day!

Your Monthly Allowance:

- 4 Servings - Red meat

Your Weekly Allowance:

- 3 Servings: Eggs, Potatoes, Sweets
- 3–4 Servings: Nuts, Olives, Pulses
- 7–14 tbsp.: Olive oil
- 4 Servings: Legumes- Poultry
- 5–6 Servings: Fish

Your Daily Allowance:

- 3 Servings: Fruit, Dairy Products
- 6 Servings: Vegetables
- 8 Servings: Non-refined products and cereals (brown rice, whole grain bread, etc.)

Olive Oil: Acts as a major added lipid

Learn Portion Control

These are general guidelines that can help you calculate the serving sizes of your meal planning:

- **Meat**: 2.1 ounces of fish or lean meat
- **Potatoes**: 3.5 ounces
- **Vegetables**: 1 cup of raw, leafy veggies or .5 cup of all others
- **Dairy**: 1 cup of yogurt or 1 cup of milk, 1.1 ounces of cheese
- **Eggs**: 1 egg
- **Grains:** .5 cup cooked rice or pasta; 1 slice of bread is almost 1 ounce
- **Nuts**: 30 grams (1.1 ounces): Sprinkled on foods for flavor or as a snack
- **Legumes**: 100 grams (1 cup) of dry cooked beans
- **Fruit**: 1 orange, 1 apple, 1 banana, 1 ounce of grapes, or 7.1 ounces of watermelon or other melons
- **Wine**: 125 ml or about a 4.2-ounce glass of a regular strength red wine

How to Maintain the Mediterranean Diet Plan

You are good to go on the Mediterranean diet—even when you're out. Most restaurants will be a reasonable choice for you while you are on this diet plan. Ask the chef to prepare your food using olive oil instead of butter. Choose to have a house salad and extra veggies or have some seafood or other types of fish for the main entree. Also, eat whole-grain bread.

One huge advantage of the Mediterranean diet is that you can be flexible. These are a few additional tips for dining out, beginning with the appetizer and then entrees, beverages, and desserts. So, let's get started.

Have a healthy snack before you leave home: One of the easiest ways to stick to your Mediterranean diet while dining out is to take the edge off your hunger. Enjoy a high-protein and low-calorie snack, such as yogurt, to help you feel full. It will help you from overeating.

Enjoy a huge glass of ice water before and during your meal. Eliminate the sugary sweet drinks. The importance of water cannot be stressed enough while you are attempting to drop the pounds since it helps keep you hydrated and steers the hunger away.

Appetizer Suggestions

Remove the temptation and ask the waiter or waitress not to bring a bread-and-butter basket to the table. If you are hungry, you may be tempted to eat more than you should. Avoid fried appetizers. Stick with steamed fish or shellfish, mixed salads, broth-based soups, or grilled veggies. Share your appetizer so that you will have a smaller portion.

Beverage Suggestions

Have a non-caloric beverage like tea, seltzer water, water, or sugar-free soda. Choose a splash of orange juice or cranberry juice in seltzer water for a fizzy surprise.

Entree Suggestions

Choose from lean pork (center-cut or tenderloin), fish, poultry, or vegetarian choices. If you are bound for red meat—choose the leaner cuts, such as flank, sirloin, filet mignon, or a tenderloin. You might also want to consider that beef will have a higher calorie and fat count. Ask for substitutes for mashed potatoes, macaroni salad, potato salad, coleslaw, or French fries. Instead, choose a side salad, steamed rice, baked potato, or steamed veggies.

Use caution with sauces. Ask if it is oil-based or if there's cream or butter in the sauce. Avoid sauces with cream, cheese, oil, or butter. Request that the sauces be served in a separate container, so you can add what is allowed. Use your fork to dip the sauce to limit the temptation of over-indulging.

Enjoy your meal by eating slowly. Ask to have the plate removed when you feel full. Eat only half of the portion or share it with a friend. You can always ask for a bag to enjoy the leftovers later. It will be an excellent lunch meal. You can also ask for half of the meal to be held in the kitchen until you are through with your meal. Once again, just remove the temptation!

Dessert Suggestions

Have a cup of coffee, cappuccino, or some herbal tea with a sugar substitute or no sugar with some skim milk. Order a dessert for everyone at the table to enjoy. Order some berries or mixed fruit.

Other Ways to Keep on the Mediterranean Plan

Pace Yourself: Try eating slower and chewing your food more thoroughly. Put your utensils down between mouthfuls to help slow you down. It will also give you time for satiety to kick in.

Eliminate all-you-can-eat buffets. This is a nightmare for portion control. Don't tempt fate if you're just beginning your new diet program. Choose a smaller plate when you go to the buffet. You can also choose a normal-sized plate or fill it half full of veggies or salad.

Consider using free apps to assist you if your goal is focused on weight loss. You have made the right choice using the Mediterranean Diet, so let's go one step further:

- My Food Diary will provide you with the nutritional facts to ensure you have the correct carbohydrates, protein, and fats in your diet plan.

- MyFitnessPal has been chosen as one of the best apps available to track your macros. It's free to download, but you can also choose to update to a premium plan for higher rates.

Understand Nutrition Labels

The bulk of the food is listed in order according to weight and are usually the first ingredients. If you don't recognize an ingredient, place it back on the shelf! Consider using products that have no more than five ingredients. The longer ingredients list is probably the result of unnecessary extras, including artificial preservatives.

The Label Explained

1. Serving information at the top: This provides the size of one serving and per container.
2. Check the total calories per serving and container.
3. Limit certain nutrients from your diet.
4. Provide yourself with plenty of beneficial nutrients
5. Understand the % of daily value section.

MEDITERRANEAN DIET COOKBOOK

Conclusion

I hope you have enjoyed each segment of your copy of *The Mediterranean Diet Cookbook*. Let's hope it was informative and provided you with a lot of useful information for your new journey to the Mediterranean lifestyle. You have over one hundred options and suggestions for your new way of eating. If you find one menu item that is not exactly what you desire, switch it with another one.

Staying busy is essential to combating food or drink cravings once you begin any new dieting technique. You need to remove the *craving* from your head, so you can break the hold it has on you. Try one or all of these suggestions. Organize your computer files; that could take a while if you are like most individuals. Write in a journal about your health goals. Catch up on your favorite hobby, or start one, like drawing or painting, to keep your hands and mind occupied. Look through some photo albums to break a smile. Call a friend and talk about anything that does not pertain to food or drinks. These are just a few of the things you can do to break the craving chain, but you get the idea.

Walk away with the knowledge learned, and prepare a feast using your delicious new recipes and meal plan. Be the envy of the neighborhood when you provide a feast at the next neighborhood gathering. Show off your skills and be proud. You can also boast how much better you feel while under the Mediterranean diet plan.

Finally, if you found this book useful in any way, a review on Amazon is always appreciated!

Made in the USA
San Bernardino, CA
08 February 2020